Personal Finance
for
Young Adults

7 Simple Steps To Gain Financial Literacy, Become Debt Free, Generate Multiple Sources Of Income, And Achieve Financial Freedom

By: Jerrell Mccain

Table of Contents

What On Earth Is Personal Finance?

"If you want to be financially free, you need to become a different person than you are today and let go of whatever has held you back in the past."
— Robert Kiyosaki

You have your whole life ahead of you.

Being young is to be full of potential. It's to have multiple, myriad paths laid out before you, all of which can be yours for the picking. All you have to do is decide upon what you want.

Being young is to be strong and resilient. You are able to get beaten back by certain things, whether they be surprisingly bad grades, a break-up with a partner, the ups and downs of young adulthood, a hard job that demands a lot but gives little, or family issues that teach you about your character. No matter what is thrown at you, you are able to bounce back and overcome it when you are young. You are able to take each and every incident and use it as an opportunity for growth and strength.

Being young is to be intuitive too. You like to go with your gut. You like to try new things, see what feels good and what doesn't, and figure out a sort of personality and way of life that you might use for decades ahead.

Being young is a lot of things but it can also be irresponsible with your money.

The sad truth is that many young people don't spend their money the right way. And save it? No, most young people don't save their money either. When it comes to personal finance, most young adults don't really think about it, worry about it, or even know about it.

Until it is too late, that is.

It's ironic that you are charged thousands upon thousands of dollars just to get a formal education in this country. But that is the sad reality that many people face every year. They enter school, they attend college, they learn all that they need to know. And then they spend the next few decades paying off the huge load of debt that they acquired.

Some people *never* pay off their student debt. And some people start to dig a big pit of debt at that young age. They are gaining all of that debt for the right reasons, they simply want to attend an institute of higher learning and be all that they can be, but they are still racked with so much debt that they can't see a way out of it.

And then they enter the real world with this number hanging over their head so they don't necessarily think about saving a lot of money. Or they are saddled with a job that only pays enough to make ends meet, no extra to save.

Maybe their parents didn't teach them much about holding a savings account or planning for the future. Maybe their rent is so high that they can't. Maybe they just don't have time to sit down, think about their financial future, and plan accordingly.

Then, before they know it, these people have no money for the future, are now in student debt *and* credit card debt, and are living in a place that is too small but too expensive to get out of.

As you can see, a descent in financial disarray can be quick, especially when you are young. You can be less than 25 years old and carry more debt and financial woes than your parents ever did.

But what if it didn't have to be that way?

The truth is that it doesn't. There are many ways for you to learn all about personal finance, even at a young age. You don't need the help of a professor or a parent, you can do it all on your own, now, with this book. You can learn what the experts have taught people for ages. These are lessons that work, things you should attain and hold onto, patterns and trends that you should follow, and pieces of advice that will not lead you down the wrong path.

Some young adults feel that learning about personal finance is boring and the opposite of fun. Who wants to learn about money? Who wants to take time to think about personal responsibility instead of having fun, being young, and living the best years of your life?

Okay, it might not be as flashy as some other areas of education or life that are out there but what it can do for you is far bigger and more important than almost anything else.

Do you want a new car in your 20s? Do you want to live in a high-rise apartment before you're 21? Do you want to be able to go on vacations, travel the world, buy the latest phone or computer or device? Do you want the best in fashion and technology and nightlife hobbies?

You can have all of that and you won't be stressed out and worried as you enjoy them all. But that is only possible if you take your destiny into your own hands and get a good, solid understanding of personal finance and what it means to you, your future, and your life.

Personal finance isn't boring, it isn't slow and dull, but it does have a huge impact on the life you live and the life you will lead 10, 20, 30 years from now. So why not study it, learn about it, and flourish?

No, personal finance isn't boring but many books about it are. Not this one. Here, we will dive into the ins and outs of this wild and exciting world of financial freedom and well-being. We will talk about where so many other people go wrong and how you will go right. We will look at your life, examine it, make it better, and set you on the right path. A path that is full of hefty paychecks, strong bank accounts, and a life that you have always wanted to live.

For years now, personal finance has been my area of expertise and I have taught a countless number of people how to take care of themselves in the most important ways. I have seen people change, even when they carry the worst habits. From 15-95 years old, I have helped people through all walks of life. I have seen the impact that a strong personal financial education can have on someone. And I am ready, and eager, to help you experience it too.

You are young and there is so much potential before you. But only if you take your life into your own hands, do what is needed, study personal finance, and then make a plan and follow it closely.

Don't worry, we will teach you about all of that. The future has never seemed so bright.

Personal Finance & You

"The question isn't at what age I want to retire, it's at what income."

— *George Foreman*

You may have heard the phrase personal finance many times before. In fact, you surely have.

You have a vague idea of what it is and you know that people say it is vital to be mastered if you wish to live a long and happy and successful life.

But do you *really* know what personal finance is? Do you know what it involves and how it manages the world that you live in? Do you know how good personal finance can present you with the best opportunities in life and how bad personal finance will only give you headaches and pain and anxiety and a lot of extra stress?

Yes, personal finance is *that* important and has *that* sort of impact. Even if you don't know what it is, it will affect you in some major ways.

So, the best way to be good at your own personal finance is to understand it, right? Knowledge is always power and you need a lot of knowledge about this subject.

Therefore, let's start with the biggest question of them all: what exactly is personal finance?

What is Personal Finance?

Think of the greatest company that you know of. The one that you respect the most, the one you can rely on constantly, the one you admire for how it is run and what it offers you.

Maybe this company is a grocery store. Maybe it's a makeup brand. Maybe it's a tech company that makes your cell phone. Whoever it is, it is a business that is being run with millions, possibly billions, of dollars.

There is a lot of money coming into this business that you are thinking of, and a lot of money going out too.

Employees need to be paid, locations need to be built and maintained, advertising needs to be created and, of course, products need to be manufactured too. You have to spend money to make money and any business worth its salt knows that.

Now, what would happen to this company that you love so much if it doesn't run well? What happens if the people running the show aren't spending correctly, what if they are paying out more than they are making, what if they aren't properly budgeting and know how much money they have in their accounts?

Well, you know what would happen then. This business would go belly up and would soon be out of business.

If a company isn't run well, it will go out of business. And when people say "run well", they almost always mean "run well financially."

But the very same is true for you and everyone else you know. You might not be a business; you might not be creating products or goods and services for people. You might just be one regular person but you can be compared to a business because if you don't handle your finances well then life will no longer be fun and carefree.

You won't be out of business like a company but you certainly won't be able to do any business.

Personal finance is simply the study and control and management of the money that you make. This isn't the money your friends or your family make. This is *your* money. How you handle it and how you take care of it and how you study it is all part of personal finance.

How you earn your money is part of personal finance. How you spend it is too. How you invest it and make it grow and how you make bets and plans for the long term with it are all part of personal finance.

It's a huge area of expertise, and there is a lot to study. Now, more than ever, mastering your own personal finance is vital.

The world is an expensive place right now. The price of just about everything keeps going up, from phones to cars to homes to more. But there are all items that you have to own at one point or another. Therefore, you will not be able to get by unless you plan accordingly and take care of your money and your finances.

This is all easier said than done. But like any subject that is worth knowing, you need to put the time and energy and effort into mastering your personal finance. This isn't something that is often taught in school - but it should be. If you can't figure this out, if you can't get this under control, if you can't handle this like an adult - despite your age - you will only face serious problems later in life.

Personal finance is the mastering of your money. Therefore, personal finance is perhaps one of the most important things in the world.

Let's dig a bit more into personal finance and what it means, by discussing some of the most important and well-regarded concepts of personal finance and how it can help you in the long run.

Top Ten Concepts of Personal Finance

There are many ways to manage your money. In fact, according to who you talk to, there are countless ways and things for you to keep in mind when you are trying to get a hold on how you make and spend your money in the long term.

The problem is that there are so many tidbits, facts, and pieces of advice floating around the world regarding personal finance that you might not know where to start.

You can get overwhelmed and daunted by the amount of stuff that is out there, especially on the internet. The web has exploded with all sorts of "experts" who say they know what they are talking about. But do they really?

Thankfully, there are several concepts and pointers that have risen above the others over the years. Through the test of time and the millions of people who have relied on them, these concepts have become popular and reliable and have become something of a proven law when it comes to personal finance.

So, what are the ten biggest concepts that you should be aware of before you start your journey of mastering your personal finance? What are the ideas that everyone agrees upon?

Budget!

You have probably heard this basic premise many times in your life. You have likely had parents, grandparents, teachers, and even friends who have said that you absolutely need to put attention into budgeting your checking and saving account all of the time.

Plan ahead, these people said. Make sure you know how much money is coming in and how much is coming out. But you never really saw the need when you were growing up and it never seemed like budgeting was something that you actually had to invest time into.

As you get older, you will soon learn that budgeting is very important. In fact, it can be make-or-break and might be the difference between making your rent payments and having to find a new place to live or a new car to drive or a new job to have.

Yes, budgeting really is that important.

Making certain that what leaves your accounts every month doesn't surpass what comes in may require budgeting and knowing how to manage your bank accounts. Relying solely on the fact that everything will work out by the conclusion of the month might result in bank fees, lots more debt, and a failure to reach your financial objectives.

By combing over your recent records and compiling a list of both your average monthly income and monthly expenses, you can quickly get control of your money.

The money that you have can be organized into groups which include necessities (such rent, utilities, and food) and expenditures (like shopping trips, traveling, going out and eating). You might wish to keep track of your expenses for about a month, using a journal or an application on your smartphone, to have a better understanding as to how your money is being spent every day.

When you are aware of all of your regular monthly inflows and outflows, you may determine whether you are sliding backwards, maintaining your current position, or, preferably, moving forward by contributing to your savings every month.

Going over your plan and looking for methods to reduce unnecessary expenditure is an excellent starting step if you aren't surviving within your limitations or you'd want to have more money available for savings. Can you eat at home more often rather than eating out? Buy fewer clothes?

Avoid Credit Card Debt!

Have you ever had a credit card before? As you get older and start living your life as a more independent young adult, you will see that credit card offers will be a-plenty and that there might be more than one that attracts you.

There is nothing wrong with that and there is certainly nothing wrong with having a credit card. It's a great way to build credit, which will help you in the future, and it's also a wonderful way to have a little extra funds to spend.

But you need to be very careful because one that easily comes with credit cards is credit card debt and you most certainly do not want that. One of the biggest problems that people make when they attempt to handle their own personal finance issues is credit card debt.

Sadly, it's also one of the easiest issues to run into and in a matter of time, you will have dug yourself a hole that you can't get out of without a lot of hard work. Some people spend years and years in serious problems with their credit card debt.

It can be alluring to spend more than you can pay if you have access to a credit card. However, maintaining a credit card balance day to day significantly increases the cost of those transactions.

The issue is that credit cards frequently have interest rates exceeding 16%, making them among the worst available. This indicates that a minor charge spread out over a number of months might easily grow to be a considerably greater sum. This also applies to other high-interest debt, including some personal or payday lenders.

But, if you currently possess debt with a high interest rate, you shouldn't be alarmed. There really are strategies for repaying that amount.

You can use credit cards, there is nothing wrong with that. You simply have to use them correctly.

Pay On Time!

Part of using a credit card smartly is paying it back with a definitive schedule. The general rule of thumb is the faster you can pay back any debt you acquire, the smarter. Credit is something you want to build, but debt is not.

There are multiple reasons why you should be paying your debts on time. For starters, it is a great way to give you peace of mind. You don't have to worry about a looming payment that is hanging over your head.

But secondly, and more importantly, if you pay on time, you will ensure that you are not going to harm your credit and ruin your chances at buying a house, a car, or renting an apartment in the future.

Another reason you want to pay on time is because if you don't, the people you owe are going to make your life very difficult, stressful, and full of worry.

Your creditors may charge fees for late payment if you skip installments or pay bills after the due date. Your accounts may become delinquent or be turned over to collectors if you put off paying for an extended length of time.

Your credit score, which borrowers will use to determine whether or not they will provide you credits and money and financing, can be impacted by delayed payment.

A record of missing or skipping payments or delayed bill payments can have a significant negative impact on your credit score because your late payments make up 35% of your credit rating. You might well have trouble getting loans with a low credit score, and the loans you do acquire will probably have higher rates of interest.

Make a note of your expenses and their payment deadlines, set up automatic pays when that is possible, and register for notifications to ensure you cannot forget one.

Build An Emergency Fund!

The sad truth is that you need money to survive just about any sort of emergency. It doesn't matter if you wreck your car, get a broken tooth, lose the air conditioning in your home, or have to suddenly fly home because of a death in the family.

All of those situations are very serious and you cannot wait around and let them pass. But you also cannot get through them without spending money. And that is exactly why one of the best, smartest basic premises behind personal finance is to always have extra money ready for moments just like this. You don't *want* to use your funds in these ways but you might have to and you will forever regret it if you're not prepared.

Being prepared really is the best way to get through these sorts of painful, stressful, heartbreaking situations.

You are young right now so you might not have much experience with situations like the ones listed above. Sadly, you will someday. And when that day comes, yes, you want to be prepared and ready to act. And that means you will need to have funds ready to help you.

You never know when your cell phone will stop working or when you'll need to go to the doctor because of an emergency. If you don't really have funds set aside for unforeseen expenses, you run the danger of accruing high-rate credit card balances or falling behind on your payments because you will need to pay for these things, there is no way around it.

You might wish to begin setting a little cash aside each month to create a rainy-day fund, or emergency fund, to prevent this from happening. No one wants to go into debt because of unforeseen, necessary spending. Between three and six months' worth of essential living expenditures should generally be kept away in a different savings account.

Save For Retirement!

You might laugh at the idea of retiring right now.

When you are young, the thought of retirement seems so far-fetched, so far away, it's like moving to Mars. It just doesn't feel like something that you need to think about.

In many ways, you don't. No, you don't need to start thinking about where you'll live or how you'll spend that time. Don't start making BINGO plans just yet! But you do need to be smart and preemptive about living your best life in your twilight years. The day *will* come when you are retiring from your job, whatever that may be, and you will feel horrible if you have nothing to rely on and lean on when it does.

The thought of having to work after you don't want to is a huge pain in the neck. If you're like other people, you probably get grumpy and upset when you have to work even 15 to 20 minutes after your shift was supposed to conclude.

Now imagine working years after you have planned to retire. Yes, that doesn't sound ideal at all.

Sadly, millions of people deal with this problem every year. They haven't budgeted correctly nor planned ahead and they have to get a job that they don't want to make money that they need. They are tired, they are wasting their time working when they should be kicking back with their spouses and loved ones and enjoying their elderly years.

Yes, early in life, retirement may seem a long way away. However, by saving cash as soon as you can, you'll have much more time to distribute it throughout your lifetime instead of trying to catch up quickly when retirement is approaching.

But the potential of compound interest may be the main justification for beginning as soon as you can. The more you save, the more you will eventually have. You don't even have to be socking away lots of money every month and it will still add up if you keep at it and don't let up over time.

Yes, tiny amounts of money will expand over time since interest is earned on both deposits and accrued interest. You might wish to think about submitting a contribution to a 401(k) or other employer-sponsored program if you have one, particularly if your workplace will match your investment.

You could be eligible to open a standard IRA, a Roth IRA, or a SEP IRA as well, dependent on your circumstances.

There are now many ways that you can start putting money away for your eventual retirement. You might be young and retiring might be a long, long way off. That's all very true. But if you want the sort of money that you'll need to really live a good and comfortable life at that point, you need to start saving soon.

You won't be saving a lot at a time and you won't even notice the little amounts going into your account usually, but you will be doing yourself a huge favor by advancing your future.

Invest!

Here is another piece of advice you've surely been given throughout your young life. There are likely numerous people who have said that you should invest in the market...or cryptocurrencies...or ETFs...or NFTs.

Yes, there are so many things to invest in that the very idea might feel downright daunting and overwhelming. And that leads to so many people missing out on investing, which honestly is a very good way to give yourself a strong financial future that is full of opportunity, financial success, and the chance to make a lot of money on small investments.

Investing is all about knowing the market that you are putting your money into. Are you investing in Wall Street stock? Maybe you are investing in foreign currencies. There are plenty of ways for you to put money and hope to get a lot more out in return. But they all require two things: commitment and education.

Yes, no matter what you are investing in, you need to study it and study it well. You will need to do research and understand what you are investing in and *why*.

Again, there are so many options when it comes to the sources that you will look to. From web message boards to newsletters to newspapers and magazines and more, there is just so much information out there about investing. Learning how to research in investing will require its own form of research.

Yes, it can be a lot as mentioned above. But it can also be so worth it.

You can select the financial institution with which you want to engage with and then establish a conventional trading account to begin investing. After this, you can place your funds in an exchange-traded fund or mutual fund that combines many sorts of assets, or, if you're willing to put some work into your study, you can select your own bonds and stocks.

It is very important that you take this form of financial freedom and opportunity seriously. Far too many people look at investing as some sort of game and don't treat it with the respect and care and attention to detail that it needs. With the invention of apps like Robinhood, it has never been easier to invest. That is a good thing. But it will be an awful thing for you if you don't take this very seriously, remain measured and smart, and don't make any huge mistakes.

Become Insured!

No one wants to think about all the risks and dangers that come with life. In fact, that is the worst thing that you want to think about. Who wants to spend their time thinking of all the ways that you might end up in the ER, or worse?

And when you are young, that is *really* the last thing on your mind. You are youthful, you are healthy, the world is your oyster and you can't get any sense of danger in your life. Your health has never been better in life so why would you need to think of looking out for it?

Some people feel invincible when they are young. And there is a reason for that because young people are surprisingly resilient and strong and seem to avoid many problems that older people do not.

But that will not always be the case. And even younger people sometimes experience situations that are not ideal and can complicate their health and their well-being in multiple ways.

That is where insurance comes in. You are quite familiar with the concept of insurance, especially if you have a car, but there are many ways that you can use insurance in your life as you grow older and this will all add to not only your financial well-being but your physical, mental, and emotional well-being too.

When disaster strikes, insurance can be the difference between good medical care and none at all, between a healthy and comfortable life and, well, the alternative.

Long-term insurance coverage and life insurance may be a wise option if you have dependents, such as children or other family members. Via their jobs, numerous individuals gain their health and disability insurance. You could also work with an insurance provider, dealer, or the insurance agency personally if you do not have that choice.

Use Credit Card Rewards!

You might think that credit cards offer you a way to buy the goods and services you desire and nothing more. You might think that would be more than enough to offer. And it is! Credit cards are a great thing that can give you many opportunities, less financial stress, and a pathway to a happy and comfortable future.

But they actually offer you more than just credit. Nowadays, credit card companies will give you so many great perks, rewards, and limited time offers that are only available to people who have signed up and received a credit card from them.

And you should take that into consideration when you are choosing the right credit card for you as a young adult.

If your credit score is good, you might want to consider applying for a credit card with incentives that could earn you cash back or miles for flights via certain airlines. If traveling is a top priority for you, you may wish to search for a credit card with flexible travel benefits, which means the points you earn can be used at a variety of airlines and hotels. You may choose to consider a credit card that provides a significant bonus upon signing and then make a certain amount of purchases within the initial months in addition to incentives. Also, preferable would be one without an annual payment.

Regardless of which card you choose, it's a sensible move to become comfortable with its loyalty program and rewards program, including its minimal redemption requirements, the value of its reward units (points, miles, or cashback offers), how to use them, and whether your rewards lapse, and how to utilize these.

The fact that credit card rates are often far greater than rewards points rates is something else you might want to bear in mind. Therefore, it might be advisable to be certain to pay your whole statement amount by the deadline each month in order to prevent having your profits eaten away by financing costs.

Choose The Right Bank!

There may be few things that sound less exciting than choosing the bank that you are going to sign up with. When you were young, your parents handled that for you. They chose the bank, set up the accounts in your name, and even invested money into them.

But you are not living with your parents anymore and now you are handling your own financial choices, including the bank that you will be signing with. And there are more choices than ever before when it comes to this decision. That is why you need to make sure that you are making the right one.

Now more than ever, there are numerous different financial organizations, all offering something new to you as a potential customer. Like any business, they are trying to attract you, woo you, bring you in and hold onto your money. They will do a lot to sign you, so it can be a smart idea to compare them to discover one that truly meets your requirements.

The types of banks that exist have grown a lot - especially over the last few years. Now, you don't just have the ones that you can walk into in person and sign up with. In fact, now you can start a bank account completely online in a matter of seconds. Lots of opportunities, obviously, but lots to be overwhelmed by too.

These days, there are online banks that you can use. These organizations often don't have any physical locations. Instead, every interaction you will have with the bank takes place online. As a result, their fees and interest rates are frequently very low. An online bank may be a fantastic choice if you do not require in-person money conversation and would rather manage your finances from home and on your phone.

Be that the financial institution you select has a consumer-friendly website and mobile app, in addition to smartly situated ATMs that won't require fees to retrieve your cash, when choosing a bank.

You have to remember that banks have grown from what they used to be into full-fledged businesses just like any other. They are going to need customers; they are going to need to attract them. You can use this to your advantage and sign up with the bank that will do the most for you. You are giving them your hard-earned cash; they should at least give you some great perks and opportunities in return.

Check Your Credit Score!

The sad and honest truth is that you can't really get by far in this world if you don't have a decent to good credit score.

It might sound shocking to think that so much hangs on that particular number, but it's true. Without a good credit score, you won't be buying a car or a house or even getting a good apartment - or sometimes even the newest smartphone.

The whole world is open to people who have great credit scores. And those who don't will only end up feeling like they have gotten the short end of the stick in just about every way.

A credit score is based upon if you pay your debts on time. If you have a credit card, you need to at least make your owed payment amount by the date that it is due. If you own a cell phone (which of course you do), you need to pay your bill on time. The same is true for a car payment and the rent that you owe your apartment complex.

If you don't make good on these promises, the bodies that are owed money can feed the information to the credit bureaus that control the numbers and, really, control how you can survive in the world. Some people have amazing credit scores past the number 700. Others are lower, much lower.

The lower you go, the less you can do. The less you'll be loaned and the less opportunities will be laid before you.

In the past, it was always really hard to know what your credit score was. Because of complex and old-fashioned rules, you could only check your score once a year and had a limited number of places that would give you a proper reading of your rating. But times have changed and now it's never been easier to get your credit score sent to you, electronically, in just seconds.

At AnnualCreditReport.com, you may obtain a credit report from the three major credit reporting companies, Equifax, Experian, and TransUnion. Before the COVID-19 epidemic, you could just perform this once annually, but now all three credit reporting companies offer free weekly credit report reviews.

Ordering a version of your report on a regular basis and checking it for mistakes or indications of fraud can be a smart option. It is advisable to get in touch with the credit bureau or the account operator as soon as you discover something incorrect and, if necessary, to submit a formal challenge if you can.

You can recognize identity theft by reviewing your reports and taking swift action to stop it. Additionally, it can assist you in ensuring that the report is free of any mistakes that might harm your credit score. If you ever intend to rent something, buy a house, or get any other kind of funding, you'll probably have to have a good credit report.

Of course, that was a lot of information but as you can see, each of those concepts will really help you build a strong bank account and a greater understanding of your personal finances.

But if you really want to start following these concepts and living a life of true financial freedom, you need to start with what is generally considered as the baseline, vital step to become a master at personal finance: saving your money.

Step 1:
Saving

"Happiness: a good bank account, a good cook, and a good digestion."
— Jean-Jacques Rousseau

There are many people - especially young people - who are turned off entirely by the idea of saving money.

Why? Well, there are plenty of reasons why people don't like to save. Firstly, it's way more to fund to *spend* money than to make and save it. There is nothing exciting about putting money away, especially if you are not going to be able to touch it for a long time.

The idea of buying things, like new cars or computers or TVs or cell phones, is more likely to get your heart racing and make you feel elated, happy, and like you're actually getting rewarded for the hard work you have committed.

But you are not going to get anywhere with your own personal finance unless you learn how to save. In fact, saving is probably the bedrock foundation to any sort of meaningful, important, and long-lasting personal finance that you want to have in your life.

And learning about saving your money now, when you are young, is perhaps the best thing that you can do. Saving your money is a habit and a trick that few people learn. They earn money, sure, but then they spend it right away.

By learning how to save your money, you are creating a future for yourself. There are multiple ways to do that - and it's important that we start with the basics.

Bank Accounts & You

The advantages of having a checking account are numerous. Among the most common is the option to use a bank card, also known as a debit card, which is useful if you might not want to handle and keep cash with you while you make purchases. If you have a checking account with your bank, you will also be able to write a check. This doesn't seem important, but you'd be shocked at how frequently you'll be requested to use or present a check, like when you are paying rent. Even though some individuals want to use credit cards to cover their daily needs, if you fail to pay off your balance and make your payments as scheduled, you run the danger of being charged penalties and interest.

Moreover, many workplaces offer the opportunity to deposit money straight into your account if you have a job. This is known as direct deposit and it has become a very popular, handy way to get your money as soon as possible on payday.

Direct deposit is also used by several government bodies to distribute benefits. Now you no longer have to sit and wait for the money to be mailed to you, then deposited, and finally cleared. Instead, direct deposit allows you to receive your money on the day that it is meant to be disbursed. When working to make payments and budget for continuing spending, this is beneficial.

Additionally, setting up an account enables you to use payment applications and pay bills online, which is invaluable for handling monthly costs such as your cell phone and utility bills. Bank accounts keep track of the money you spend and how you spend it. This can help you stick to a budget, prevent identity theft, or uncover suspicious transactions. They are occasionally necessary when applying for a loan for expensive purchases like a house.

Is there a compelling argument against having a bank account? Nope, there really isn't. Even though some bank clients could periodically run into problems with charges, managed services, or other concerns, the advantages of having a checking account much exceed the dangers. By preserving your balance, granting you convenient access to it, and linking you with other financial services, owning a bank or credit union account may assist you to position yourself for financial security and success.

Why Should You Have A Bank Account?

You now know all the benefits of having a bank account. In many ways, there aren't any downsides to opening an account at the bank of your choosing.

But if you were to sum up the best reasons to open an account as succinctly as possible, there are a few factors that should be thought of. Without further ado, here is the best way to sum up why you should open your checking and saving account at the bank.

They Are Safe

Let's be honest: no one wants to lose their money. You worked hard for your funds! You go to your job, you do your best, you have earned it.

Plus, you can't really get by without the money that you have accumulated. If you lost all of your money overnight, you wouldn't be able to pay rent, make a payment for your car, buy your groceries, and so much more. You would be paralyzed and your life would be completely on hold.

You need your money to be safe at all times, free of people who will steal it away, spend it all, and leave you stranded without a dime. And when you open an account at a bank, you can rest assured that your cash is as safe as possible.

If you store your money at home without the protection of a bank, then you run a huge risk of it being stolen away or possibly lost. But that isn't the case when you use a bank and their protections. They are insured by the federal government to make sure that your money will remain in one place, ready for you to withdraw and use at a moment's notice.

This wasn't always the case. There was a time decades ago when the money in banks wasn't supervised and looked out for by the government. But following the Great Recession, the American government started the FDIC.

Customers can feel secure knowing their cash is secure with the help of banks and credit unions. In truth, in the unlikely chance that the bank you're working with collapses, if you open an account at a bank or credit union, you'll be covered by the FDIC or National Credit Union Association (NCUA) up to an amount of $250,000.

You are more susceptible to unexpected expenses if you keep your cash outside of bank accounts. For instance, if you only hold money in secret places throughout your house, you won't have several choices if that cash is ever taken, misplaced, or damaged.

Furthermore, not having a bank account may restrict your lending alternatives and make you more susceptible to unscrupulous, predatory, and fraudulent lenders that demand exorbitant interest rates and lock borrowers into risky debt cycles.

Additionally, banks have worked hard to keep their security strong and intact, despite the growing threat of cyber terrorists who are looking to rip people off.

The sad truth is that there are more threats than ever before when it comes to dangers that lurk online and throughout the technological age that we live in. But banks have been on the cutting edge of cybersecurity, sure to not allow these hackers and scammers to break into your account and take your money.

They Can Help Your Credit Score

As has been mentioned before, you're not going to be able to get far in this world unless you have a credit score that reflects your commitment to paying your bills on time and always living up to your expectations when it comes to your financial obligations and responsibilities.

And the good news is that opening a bank account can help with that. Yes, having a bank account might be able to help improve your credit score, which will definitely help you in the long run and will pave the way for you to be a car owner, home owner, and successful and comfortable person for most of your life.

If you have an empty credit score or if it's been hurt by any sort of late payments or negative actions against it, a bank account will give you a leg up and help you get back on track. You can use your account to pay your bills and set up automatic payments directly from it.

This will have an impact the credit bureaus will indeed notice that you are paying your obligations on time and are making good on the promises you make to credit card companies and other financial institutions.

This will all positively reflect on your credit file and you will see that, over time, your credit score will start to inch up. Now, you need to keep in mind that repairing a damaged credit score doesn't happen overnight. This takes a good amount of time and you need to ensure that you are going to stay on the right path, not slip back into bad habits, and start missing payments again.

The truth is that getting your credit score back on track is nearly impossible without a bank account. If you are looking to finally look like a good customer and a reliable member of society with a credit score that is good, you need a bank account that is active and ready to pay off the debts and obligations that you owe.

You Can Get Benefits

There was a time when signing up for a bank account was as simple as can be - and honestly, quite boring too. You would walk into the bank of your choosing, give them your personal information, sign up and put money into your account, and then your account would be active.

All pretty straight forward and bland, huh?

Oh, how times have changed.

Now when you go into a bank with the idea of opening an account, you are going to be treated as a possible customer who can bring the bank money.

Banks have changed - a lot - over the years and now they want as many customers as possible, just like any business does. They want this so they can take the money from customers and invest it into local businesses and make revenue via them. It's a whole complicated plan but the bottom line is this: banks are now businesses like the other ones you use. They need customers, they need their money, and they will do what it takes to attract them.

That means that signing up for a bank account may now come with many perks, benefits, and special limited time offers that will be attractive and entice you to sign. Maybe you will get benefits at local restaurants, maybe you will get reward points that accumulate over time and can be spent online in a variety of ways. There are so many ways that a bank might sweeten the pot and bring new customers in.

Yes, you can get a whole lot more from a bank than simply an account these days.

That is why you need to shop around when you are looking to open your bank account. Don't just agree to the first bank you come across. Instead, you should see what the alternatives offer you.

If the banks are going to try and woo you, let them. Lean into it, embrace it. Allow them to pull out all the stops and show you the bells and whistles they will lay before you in order to secure your business.

Are Bank Accounts Free?

There are several solutions which don't force you to maintain some sort of minimum balance in your checking or savings account, although it's accurate many do. Consult a salesperson at your bank about your alternatives and obtain a clear knowledge of any fees before you start an account.

Nevertheless, not owning a bank account may potentially be expensive. For instance, if you don't own and maintain an account, you'll need to find ways to remind yourself to pay each bill directly and run the risk of incurring service charges.

If you're similar to most people, your life just gets very hectic, therefore it's not unusual to forget to make a payment every once in a while, or to submit them late. Sadly, there are extra penalties and fines for making a payment past the due date that was agreed upon. If you keep track of your outstanding balance, what is being withdrawn, and when, the option to establish automatic payments is a wise method to keep a good handle on your finances.

Certain checking accounts might offer overdraft protection, that allows your bank to pay the difference if the balance falls under zero due to movements for a fee.

What Is The Difference Between A Savings & Checking Account?

When you look at all the services provided by a bank, you might be a bit overwhelmed and that is completely understandable. As banks have grown over the last few decades, so have the number of products that they sell and bring to customers.

There are numerous distinct categories of bank accounts. Checking and savings accounts are the most popular types of accounts that will be offered to you at the bank. That is because a diverse set of financial demands and objectives are taken care of from each account. While a bank can help you set up a number of other types of accounts, these two will always be the ones that bring in the most customers.

You may be wondering what the difference between a checking and savings account is. Which one is more important? Should you get one or both? And how do they work and how do they affect each other?

Your cash can be accessed quickly through checking accounts. The debit card gives you virtually immediate access to your funds regardless of whether you're at home or out and about.

The ability to produce electronic payments via bill pay, a function provided by checking accounts, is yet another advantage. You can enable automated payments for your bills with many banks, allowing you to schedule payment installments that will work on their own and give you peace of mind. This might save you from late fines and other costs. If you decide to set up automatic bill payment, ensure the account is never depleted of funds to prevent additional any inadequate fund fines, something your bank will impose if you take out more funds than you may have on hand.

So, what about savings accounts? In which situations are they the ideal account to have?

When creating an emergency savings for specific objectives, savings accounts are the way to go. Savings account interest rates are often greater than those on checking account interest rates. Since holding onto your money and watching the value of your funds grow over time is the main goal of a savings account, certain large banks may impose a monthly transaction cap.

This means that you might get charged a small fee if you move money from your savings account to another more than a few times a month.

Banks might also require that you keep a minimum amount in your savings at all times too.

You might be given the option to establish what is known as a high-yield account, a certificate of deposit, or a money market profile while creating a bank account. As a result, you receive a larger return on your investment from these accounts than you would from a conventional savings account.

At the end of the day, the best way to look at checking and savings accounts is that one of them is used to pay bills, buy groceries, and get you through your day-to-day life (checking). Meanwhile, one account is used to store and save your money and let it grow over the years with interest (savings).

While both of these accounts will have their own respective fees and regulations based upon the bank that you are using, the savings account is typically more strictly monitored and regulated and you will likely have to follow the rules of the bank a bit closer because they really want you to keep your stored safely and soundly in your savings account without much movement or change.

So, which one should you choose? The honest answer is simple: both. Ideally, you will be able to set up both a checking and savings account at the same bank. Just ask one of the tellers working and they will be more than happy to get you set up. This helps them out (it brings them business and money) and it helps you out too, because it will set you up for a financially successful future.

You will learn that one of the most important aspects of personal finance when you are a young adult is planning ahead and laying the groundwork for the future years. This might seem silly or unnecessary but trust me when I say you should always start planning young.

A savings account is a great way to plan young. What a savings account does is, well, *save*. You will not be spending the money that you put into your savings account but you will let it grow and develop and become so much more over the years. Set it and forget it and let it grow naturally and healthily.

Meanwhile, you will be using your checking account to buy what you need and live your life. And, if you want to add money from your checking account to your savings account, you certainly can. But you should try to not send money in the opposite direction, as banks will limit the number of times you can take money out of your savings account.

Both a checking and savings account together are a great way to get a solid handle on your personal finance. They are not the first step to a successful financial life but they are a great start.

Saving your money is essential because you can't have it if you don't hold onto it. And, thankfully, it's never been easier to save your money because there are so many banks, so many financial institutions, and so many enticing reasons to sign up for them.

Now, what is one of the most important things to know when you are trying to save your money? Budgeting, of course. It's the key to holding onto and saving your money, even with the common expenses that you have to account for.

Next Steps

So, what should you do if it's time for you to open a bank account? The good news is that it's never been easier.

You should go out into the world, take a look at the big banks in your area, and see what they have to offer. Like when you shop for a new cell phone, you should go into one of these banks, ask some questions, see what they have to offer, and figure out how they will try to make you a customer. Let them woo you - that's their job and it will only benefit you more.

There are surely multiple banks located near your home and they are each ready and willing to show you what they have to offer. Choose the one that is right for you, bring the necessary documentation, and you will soon have your very own bank accounts set up.

Step 2:
Budgeting

Few words instantly bore people more than "budgeting".

For something that is so universally necessary, needed, and employed by the most successful people all over the world, budgeting sure doesn't have a lot of fans.

Why? Because people find themselves entirely bored and turned off by the concept of budgeting. Think about it and it certainly doesn't sound that fun: sitting down, looking at the money you make and the amount you spend and then finding ways to make both of those numbers healthier? No, that doesn't sound like the best way to spend an afternoon.

However, that's not a real good evaluation and representation of what budgeting is. Instead, budgeting is actually a very helpful tool that can work wonders for you, especially if you're young.

No, budgeting isn't crunching numbers. There is so much more to it than just that.

In reality, budgeting is about setting goals for yourself. It's about rewarding yourself, honestly. With budgeting, you can set your eyes on the ultimate prizes. You can find ways to get that new car, buy that new cell phone, move into the apartment that you have always dreamed of. There are so many things you can achieve when you take budgeting seriously.

Budgeting is simply looking at how much money you have, how much you spend, and making a plant that will get you from point A to point B as easily and smartly as possible. That's really the long and short of it, it doesn't get much simpler than that.

Yet, still, so many people don't see the value in budgeting. Young people are especially bad about thinking ahead and making financial plans for themselves. And because of that, they miss out on so many opportunities.

So, let's really discuss budgeting and show you why it's something you should spend your time, energy, and effort on. It really shouldn't be looked at as a dirty word because few things are as helpful or rewarding as putting together a good budget, sticking to it, and reaping the rewards.

Why Do You Need A Budget?

A budget enables you to identify and strive toward your overall objectives. How are you going to accumulate enough cash to purchase a car or make a down payment on a home if you just float mindlessly throughout existence, throwing your cash at any attractive, sparkly product that seems to catch your attention?

A plan like a budget compels you to identify objectives, save cash, monitor your progress, and realize your aspirations. Okay, so it could be painful to learn that the hotly-anticipated new PlayStation game or the exquisite silk blouse are out of your price range. But it will be a lot simpler to turn around and leave the store empty-handed if you remind yourself that you are saving money for a new house.

Before the advent of debit and credit cards, people were much more aware of their financial situation. If they had sufficient funds at the conclusion of a month or pay period to cover their expenses and put a little away for savings, they had been on the right track. Nowadays, people who misuse their credit cards often don't become aware of their buying habits until they're in serious debt.

But if you make and follow a budget, it is unlikely that you'll ever be in this perilous position. Instead, you'll be fully aware of your earnings, your monthly spending capacity, and your required savings amount. It's true that budgeting and figure crunching aren't nearly as entertaining as mindless shopping. Now consider this: on this day next year, when your frivolous pals are scheduling a debt counseling session, you'll be flying off on a vacation you've been collecting money for, or maybe you'll have that flashy new computer you want or the cherry car you have been longing for.

Assume you manage your finances well, stick to your spending plan, and never accrue credit card debt. Bravo for you! But don't you seem to be missing something? Saving money is essential for your future, just as it is crucial to use your money sensibly today.

You can achieve that by using a budget. Including investing contributions in your budget is crucial. You can eventually accumulate a comfortable nest egg if you set aside a percentage of your income each month to put into your IRA, 401(k), or any other retirement accounts. And although you may need to make some sacrifices today, it will be worthwhile in the long run. Which would you prefer: working as a hostess at a local restaurant to pay your bills and get by, or playing golf and visiting the beach in your old age? As you can see, the choice is obvious.

Random and sudden surprises abound in life, some of which are greater than the others. Financial hardship might result from losing your job, getting sick or hurt, getting divorced, or experiencing a family member's death. Of course, it feels like these situations usually happen when you least expect them. In other words, they seem to always happen when you already have a tight budget. For precisely this reason, everybody requires an emergency fund.

An emergency reserve that covers a minimum of around three to six months' worth of spending should be included in your budgeting plan. After a crisis in your life, this extra cash will ensure that you don't fall further and further into debt. Of course, saving up three to six months' worth of costs will take time.

Try not to immediately deposit the bulk of each pay period into your emergency savings. Create a budget for it, make clear objectives, and begin small. This emergency fund should gradually increase even if you only set aside $10 to $30 per week. Based on your strategy, budgeting applications like Mint or YNAB offer tools for creating an emergency fund.

You are forced to examine your spending patterns after creating a budget. You might discover that you're shelling out cash on goods you don't require. If you have a pricey extended cable plan or numerous streaming subscriptions, do you really watch all of the channels that you have? Do you need THAT many Starbucks drinks every week? Do you have to eat out so often? You can reevaluate your spending patterns and concentrate your financial goals by using a budget.

Based on the person, there are several justifications for having a budget. A budget can frequently aid in achieving monetary autonomy and freedom. A budget can help you reach your financial objectives, live inside your means, save for retirement, create an emergency savings, and track your spending patterns.

Tips For Budgeting

Online Tools

There was a time when the only way to make a budget was to sit down, get out your checkbook, a bunch of receipts, and get to work.

Well, times have changed. Thanks to the invention of the internet and all the websites that have come with it, you now have plenty of tools that allow you to work on budgeting all from the comfort of your bed and the ease of a touchscreen smartphone.

Try utilizing online tools that can monitor your expenses and income to maintain tabs on your budget. These programs provide a simple method for setting up a budget. It's important to know your earnings and where your money goes. These tools could make it easier for you to identify areas where you can make savings and where your money is going.

You may construct a budget, keep track of your revenue and expenses, and establish savings objectives using the free online program called Mint. Weekly reports will be delivered to your email to allow you to monitor your spending.

You Need a Budget, also known as YNAB, is a different alternative to look into even though it may seem illogical to spend money on budgeting software while trying to reduce your spending. It can assist you in creating a budget, put money away for unforeseen bills, and create a rainy-day fund.

Giving every dollar a job, accepting your genuine spending, rolling with the punches, and maturing your money are the four guiding principles of YNAB. Either $11.99 per month or $84 annually are required.

Automate Your Savings

It is awfully tempting to *not* save and stick to your budget when you are manually making all the moves inside your accounts. When you are the one transferring the money, you run the risk of deciding to instead withdraw the money or spend it or just not stick to the plan that you have created.

But when you take yourself out of the equation, budgeting well and improving your savings account is far easier.

Consider automating at least monthly withdrawals out of your checking account into a savings account also in your name. Saving about 10% or 20% of your salary is a typical goal, but if it seems like a lot, try to start with 1% and gradually increase that number over time. You may preset it and ignore it if you can survive on slightly less. Out of sight, out of mind, and without the chance of you dipping into the money you are saving.

To estimate how much you can expect to save, experts advise taking a look at the monthly income and spending. How would you go about doing this?

If you get paid twice per month and then have $200 in excess each month, instruct your bank to transfer $50 from each paycheck to the savings account. You are less tempted to spend because you rarely see the money arrive in your checking account.

Be Realistic About Budgeting

We are all human and things happen that often create speed bumps and get in the way of following the plan exactly as you wanted. Things happen! Even the best laid plans sometimes go slightly off track. You need to consider this and accept it but never lose faith and get too far off the path you have created for yourself.

Making a budget is difficult. At many times, it seems like a severe diet that is incredibly hard to stick to. Being realistic is essential for creating an effective budget and for saving money.

To put it another way, make an effort to leave money in your budget for the things you value, such as entertainment. If you have to make big changes, think about gradually reducing your consumption and indulging in moderation.

You likely won't be able to totally change your spending patterns overnight, just like you can't completely change your dietary behaviors. Your necessities, wants, and savings can all be taken into account in a well-balanced budget.

Budget For Extra Spending

If only everything went according to plan. Budgeting is planning, yes, and sometimes your plan needs to account for the things you didn't see coming. Because life is known to throw a few curveballs at all of us, it's smart to make sure that you keep these in mind, even if you don't know what they will be. The particulars might end up being vague but you can plan accordingly and make sure that all your bases will be covered, even when the curveballs are bigger than usual.

Unexpected expenses, like auto repairs or medical bills, might be one of the things that prevent people from sticking to their budgets. Even routine costs like yearly insurance premiums or tax payments can surprise you.

Budgeting is typically simpler for recurring monthly costs like rent, meals, and transport. But we all have expenditures that are difficult to plan for, and it's possible that we won't remember them until the bill is due or we receive a significant shock.

Contemplate creating a new section in your budget to serve as a safety net for these costs in order to solve the situation. In this circumstance, create an emergency fund.

Every Month Is Different

Just like the warm, beautiful summer months of the year are different from the cold, inviting winter ones, so too will your budget change depending on the season and the months that you are in.

You'll need to set aside money in certain months for items like school supplies or standard auto maintenance. You'll be setting aside money at other times for stuff like trips, anniversaries, and celebrations.

No matter the occasion, be sure to account for those costs in your budget. By opening your calendars as you're drafting your budget, you may prevent these special occasions from creeping up on you and doing great damage to the budget that you are creating and trying to stick to.

As circumstances change, make careful to modify your budget each month. Create a savings account that you can use to store money all year. Stress is inevitable when you don't have a plan. And that eliminates the entire joy of gift-giving and celebration. That is something that literally no one desires.

Track Yourself

You won't know how well you are doing with your budget and planning unless you sit down every once in a while, realistically and honestly look at all you have achieved and where you have fallen short. By doing this, you can keep track of yourself - and reward yourself too!

It's crucial to periodically assess your development. If you're in a committed relationship, sit down and discuss your objectives. Contact someone to keep in touch with if not.

When you are discussing your budget with whoever this is - spouse or someone else - talk about how setting a budget has aided your progress. Consider ways to save costs or perhaps even find more money to help you reach your goals more quickly. And remember to recognize even the little victories.

If you have been doing really well, you should put away a little extra cash to treat yourself. Maybe it's a nice movie, maybe it's a fancy dinner. Maybe it's a night out on the town with a loved one. If you can afford it and if you've been sticking to your plan then you deserve it and this should really be something that you do regularly.

You cannot reward yourself too often but if you have had months and months of good, hard work and success, don't you deserve a treat? You know you can afford it at that point, right?

How To Make A Budget

So, now you can see all the great ways that a budget can really help your financial future and your personal finance. This is an expert approach to making sure that you are planning ahead and really laying the groundwork for a long and successful life.

But it's not as easy as just sitting down and typing up a few things and, boom, your budget is done. You need to put a lot more effort and work and time into making a real budget. By doing so, you will ensure that all your bases are covered, you're not leaving anything out, and your budget plan is set to succeed and really deliver everything that you need.

If you are ready to take the next step and actually formulate the budget that you are going to be following for the weeks, months, and years ahead, there are a few things you need to do. Thankfully, these steps are really quite easy, as long as you have the necessary information and items on hand.

Step One: Get All Your Statements Together

You require your financial data in order to start personal budgeting. Perhaps going into your bank account will provide you with all the details you require, or perhaps you will need to obtain paper statements. Get a whole years' worth of records, if you can. Gather whatever you are able to if you do not have documents that reach back that far.

Step Two: Record All Of Your Income

Examine your records, and make a list of all your income sources. Without knowing how much money you are bringing in each month, you cannot create a budget. Instead of your total compensation, note your net pay. Your "take home pay" is your net salary. It is the amount that is actually put into your bank account after taxes, perks, and any 401K contributions have been taken out by your employer. Don't forget to list any recurring revenue sources.

Even include side jobs you have that earn you money each month. Don't include it if the revenue is only occasional. You should review your records and determine your typical monthly income if you have a job that pays commissions or if your compensation fluctuates monthly.

Step Three: List Your Expenses

List out and write down all of your regular monthly costs and debt commitments, such as rent, mobile phone, car, personal loan as well as student loans, apparel, and other expenditures. You could classify dining out, socializing with pals, as well as other minor, irregular spending as "odds and ends." You ought to examine those costs closely. Many folks don't understand what they're spending on those products because the expense might creep up on them.

Don't forget to add any bills that might not be paid every month. Several regions receive sewer and water bills every two months instead of every one month. Two times a year, personal property taxes are levied in several states. Keep in mind your yearly obligations, such as the renewal of your driver's license or vehicle registration. Additionally, make sure to list any medical expenses you have, any streaming services you have access to, and any merchant automated shipments you hold.

Lastly, don't forget to reward yourself. Include the amount of money you currently contribute each month to a savings account. If not, you should check to see if your spending plan enables you to deposit the cash into an account that gains interest over time. This will now be known as your emergency fund as well as/or your fund for major objectives. To this, you need quick access. For this, try allocating 5% of your salary. This figure might fluctuate as you create your plan, yet it is a fantastic place to start.

Fixed & Variable Expenses

Look over your list of expenses and make a note of any that repeat each month or that you anticipate continuing for a while. If you enter into a new lease for an apartment, your rent can increase, but you can expect it to stay the same for the duration of your present lease.

Most consumers can anticipate that the cell phone bill won't change from month to month unless they have a data overdraft. Additionally, car and school loan repayment plans frequently remain consistent over a lengthy period. These are recurring monthly costs.

Not every bill is a recurring cost, however. For instance, when you run the air conditioner in the summertime and the heater in the wintertime, your electricity bill is going to rise. Depending on your water usage, your utility cost will change every billing cycle. Determine the average bill amount by reviewing your data for the previous year for these payments. You will include the typical amount for a variable bill in your financial plan.

If your monthly power bill is $100 but you only need to pay $70 since it's a mild spring month, for instance, send the power company $70 and save the other $30 in an account that generates interest. Even though that $30 might not yield significant interest, it will definitely help. It is money you didn't have before, no matter how small the amount. You'll have the funds in the account to make up the difference if your bill increases in another part of the year.

Step Four: Total Your Income & Expenses

You truly start learning how to manage your money at this point in the process, so listen up and buckle down because here comes the hard work. Add up the income you make in one month and also write down all the outgoing expenses you are aware of.

Write all this down and put the two columns side by side. Your revenue should be greater than your outgoing expenditures.

You get what is known as a budget surplus if your income exceeds your outgoings. Your excess will indicate whether you have enough money to pay for a newer car, a larger residence, or to make additional payments on your debt. Or you can even buy yourself something nice although it is important not to go crazy with spending.

On the flip side, a budget deficit is if your spending is higher than your revenue. Even while being in this situation is unpleasant, it is not hopeless.

Examine your financial records and come up with ways to cut costs. Can you limit your eating out? Consider purchasing food in bulk to reduce your monthly shopping expense. Do you need to look into additional cheap housing options? You might be able to get two jobs. You can decrease the amount you place into your savings account if you have to. Saving even 1% of your income is greater than none and will come in handy.

Step Five: Create Your Goals

After making lifestyle changes to create a surplus, you must decide what you want to do with your extra cash.

What are you doing in life right now? Are you residing by yourself for the first time and aware that the vehicle you've had for years won't survive very much longer? Are you contemplating a home purchase, settling down, and beginning your dream of having a family? Do you wish to open an investing account with your spare money or utilize it to reduce your debt?

The majority of financial consultants advise clients to save three months' worth of spending in savings in case of emergencies like job loss. Multiply the sum of your expenses by three. You want to have that much revenue in the savings account. Even if it can take some time to get there, you'll be glad you have it afterwards. That ought to be your first objective. Any additional savings target ought to be over that sum.

How do you accomplish your goal now that you've selected it? Say you intend to purchase an automobile within two years. You understand you may make the scheduled payments on a $15,000 car now that you understand how to put together a household budget, so you do.

Calculate your monthly payment before deciding whether to buy the car. Set up an automated plan with the bank if it falls within your spending limit and include it on the "expenses" list you made while creating your budget. Automated savings programs can assist you in staying on track with your goals by keeping you focused on your plan.

Consider your end goals whenever you're tempted to withdraw money from your savings to pay for something. Which is more necessary? Do you really want to pull money out of your account or do you really, really want that car that you are aiming to buy? The answer should be obvious.

Step Six: Review

It doesn't matter how good a plan is, it needs to be reviewed from time to time to make sure that it's really working to the best of its abilities. Even people who have been budgeting for years and do so for a living will continually check their plans and tweak them too. A budget is going to last for a long time but it will need to be changed and that will only happen if you regularly review what you have done.

The rising cost of food or an unplanned illness are outside of our control. Each month, review your spending plan. Your expenses: have they changed? Your income: has it changed? Are you going overboard with your other expenditures? You may stay inside your budget by comparing your actual spending to your planned spending.

Whenever you evaluate your plan, consider whether it is still relevant. Did you relocate or change jobs? Do you have a newborn on the way? Have you had to upgrade your car sooner than you had anticipated? Do you believe your objective no longer serves your interests? Your financial planning needs to adapt as life does.

Conclusion

See, budgeting isn't nearly as hard as you'd imagine. It's also not nearly as boring either. While maybe some aspects of it aren't the most exciting thing in the world, the overall purpose and goals of budgeting are actually quite exciting because they can lead to some amazing things.

Most of the time, the people who have the best cars on the block didn't just stumble upon them. They didn't just fall into their laps. The people worked for the money, made a plan to save the money, and then got what they wanted.

Making the plan *is* budgeting. It's a way to keep the hard-earning money that you have and to use it in the best ways possible.

It can be time consuming and, yes, sometimes a little dry and boring. But creating a budget when you are a young adult is a great way to get ahead of everyone else that you know. Your friends might be struggling to get by, living paycheck to paycheck and not able to go out and enjoy themselves with nice meals, new products, and the sort of lifestyles they really and truly want.

But that won't be you. Because you have budgeted, you will be doing exactly what you want, when you want it - all without the fear of running out of money and not being able to get by.

It takes work, but it's worth it. Few things are as important as a good, reliable budget.

Next Steps

Now that you know what you need to keep in mind, what you need to look for, and what you need to practice, you should start making a budget today. Do not wait.

With the invention of online banking and smartphones, it has never been easier to compile all of your income in an easy-to-read fashion and then get to work at making the budget that will give you the sort of life that you want.

Start by formulating a list of all the monthly expenditures you have and also add up all the money you have coming in every month into your account. This is step number one. Then start to plan for the month ahead, what you know you will be buying, and add and subtract to see what adjustments might be necessary.

Additionally, browse the app store on your phone to look for any handy budgeting applications you can add to your phone. Test them out, see which ones feel right, and stay to employ those too.

You have earned your money and now it is time to make sure you have as much of it as possible. That is where budgeting comes in and luckily you now know how to do it.

And budgeting can also help with one of the most dreaded, damaging, and scary things that can impact your personal finances and your future: debt.

Step 3:
Paying Off Debt

"Debt is the slavery of the free."
— *Publilius Syrus*

Debt.

Few words strike fear into the hearts of people more than that one. Debt can be very scary. In fact, debt can be downright terrifying.

Why?

Because if you have accumulated a lot of debt, it might feel impossible to get out of. And the truth is, sadly, it sometimes is. There are some amounts of debt that become too much.

People literally cannot make their ways out of it and they are led to declare bankruptcy or fall into a hole even deeper that they will never climb out of.

Debt can stick with you all your life. Despite what some people say, it will not go away and it will follow you around like a black cloud of your head. Do you want that new car? Well, your debt will prevent that. What about that fancy apartment that is in the perfect part of town? Sorry, it's too rich for your blood. What about a vacation or fancy dinner with friends? You really can't because you need to be paying attention to paying off your debts.

See, debt can really disrupt everything and send your life into a tailspin.

There are millions of people all over the world in billions and billions of dollars of debt. There are many causes for their debts and many things that got them to the places they are. But the one thing they all have in common is this: each and every one of them wishes they weren't in debt.

You don't want to be one of those people. And you don't have to be! While everyone will accumulate at least some debt in their lives, there are smart ways to manage, maintain, and pay them off so they don't weigh down your future and shut all the doors you want open.

Debt is scary and you should be afraid of it. But you should never be so afraid that you don't confront it. Overcoming debt *is* possible, if you know what to do.

How Do Most People Go Into Debt?

No one grows up thinking, "Hey, someday I want to get into a lot of debt that I cannot control. I want to not be able to buy new cars, new homes, or the newest and greatest items because I am burdened by a mountain of debt."

Yes, debt is the last thing that most people want and many work really hard to avoid accumulating any, yet they still do.

That's an uncomfortable truth that everyone should come to terms with: nearly everyone is going to gain some sort of debt over the years. Some people will do this because they go to school, others because they have a medical issue that needs addressing. Others are a bit more careless and make mistakes that gravely cost them - literally. For years, people have suffered from the choices they made in the past. No matter what sort of decisions you make, that sort of fate isn't fair.

A lot of people have debt but a lot of people don't *keep* their debt, and that is the big difference. Knowing how to manage the debt that you gain and how to get rid of it entirely is the difference between not being able to make ends meet and having an exciting and successful life that is filled with vacations, easy spending, and a carefree attitude.

Before we can discuss *how* to handle your debt, we need to look into the most common ways that people get into financial trouble in the first place!

Biggest Reasons Why People Experience Debt

Credit Cards Get The Best Of Them

People have different backgrounds. They grow up in a wide variety of families with distinct values and lessons that they teach - or don't teach - about spending, saving, and anything related to finance. And this will have a direct impact on the way that young people in their family spend money.

Yes, everybody has a different set of interests and deeply held values and views, the majority of which are directly related to money. And when life has certain demands and wants, people will attempt to solve them with different approaches.

Cultural views about wealth, lending, and buying influence how a person responds to not being able to satisfy wants and needs. While some people choose to wait and save money, others may crave immediate satisfaction.

And with the invention of credit cards, many people have found a shortcut to getting what they want and need. Credit cards fundamentally altered society. People might immediately gratify their wants and requirements while deferring having to make the necessary financial arrangements until later. In order to delay having to figure out how to pay for the items, many consumers sought that instant satisfaction through retail therapy made possible by those tiny plastic cards.

The truth is that people all over the world have taken the easy path to getting what they want and that easy path often involves spending a lot and not in the smartest ways. Credit cards are just part of the problem. There are countless people who just don't spend smartly - and this will end up biting them in the end.

Bad Money Management

You were probably in high school not too long ago. Ask yourself this: how many classes and how much time did you spend learning about how to save and spend your money? If you're like the vast majority of people, you didn't spend *any* time with that subject matter.

Money management just isn't taught to the vast majority of young people in this country or many others. Because of that, these students become adult members of society and they are at a loss at sometimes the simplest aspects of personal finance.

You can't really blame these people. How are they supposed to master money management if they don't know the first thing about it?

There are solutions to this of course. Yes, you might not have learned a lot about personal finance when you were going through school, but it's never too late to learn. Before you become overwhelmed by your debts, take control of them. To determine what you are spending any money on and how much of your income covers your outgoings, examine your financial records and keep a purchasing diary.

If you discover that you are squeezed too thin, try to reduce your spending or determine whether changing your phone, electricity, or even mortgage could save you money.

Negative Thinking

It is said that we are our own worst enemies and truer words have never been spoken. We all have those voices in our heads that tell us we aren't enough, aren't doing well, are imposters who don't deserve success. It can be hard to combat negative thinking when it's inside your own head.

When we start to make mistakes with money, we usually mentally punish ourselves. Instead of coming up with a plan to get through it, we instead double-down on feeling bad and convince ourselves that it's our fault and any solution isn't possible, and that we aren't even worthy of it.

We usually get really hard on ourselves and tell ourselves that we deserve the debt and can manage to repay over time when we choose to take on debt. And then we make worse mistakes, in order to *try* to make us feel better. People will give into the pricey act of buying a $15,000 car, thinking it could improve our moods and maybe give us a happier, better perspective.

This debt is manageable because it will only cost $250 a month for the following four years, we say to ourselves, and we will also satisfy our emotional needs.

For individuals with sufficient resources to cover those payments, that may turn out nicely. Others, though, can feel buyer's remorse when they see how much and how long they have to start repaying.

At that point, stress and regret are intensified by the debt. Additionally, it could make them feel trapped in a job they dislike because they need the money from it to pay off their debt, which could add to their stress.

It's Accepted

When you think of the most successful people in the world, what is one thing they all have in common? It's clear: a big bank account. Nowadays, you can't really be considered a big deal and a big success unless you have a lot of money to your name. You need to be buying the latest and greatest and jet-setting all over the world in the nicest clothes with the greatest tech if you want to be considered a true success.

This isn't new. In fact, it's a tale as old as time. Money has long been associated by society with privilege, acceptance, and social standing. Because of the perceived competence and performance skills that are intrinsically linked to individual wealth, individuals with much more money are frequently seen as more attractive and successful and, frankly, cool.

Many people have constructed a veneer supported by a pile of debt in an effort to achieve this position for themselves. They think and expect that if their apparent wealth rises, their friends and others will embrace them more on a social level. Social media, in some ways, supports and fuels this urge to appear hip, wealthy, and cool even if it costs you money that you will have to pay back later - if you can.

The Media

And how is it that is causing us to think that we can only be a success if we have a lot of money? Well, the media of course. For years now, they have been perpetuating the concept that the best and greatest people in society are those who are making and spending a lot.

Many social forces have contributed to the perception that it is okay to accumulate debt since so many venues emphasize influencers who promote things. They accept the advertising spin.

Strategic media use by brands helps them have a bigger impact on society as a whole. People consequently start to persuade themselves that they require these items in order to live happy lives.

The Economy

Although it is encouraging to see property prices climb, unemployment rates decline, and economic security rise, these changes can also give folks a false sense of security that leads them to begin taking on additional debt. This consumer confidence mentality encourages individuals to spend more, often well beyond their means, as opposed to making the decision to save more.

People have fallen victim to this trap in the past by taking out house equity loans and credit lines to purchase boats and other luxury items, only to be severely hurt when the financial bubble collapses. Home values have decreased as a result, which has put those individuals in grave danger.

They will surely find themselves underwater, with a debt that considerably exceeds the worth of their home. Insolvency and other monetary losses, such foreclosure, may result from this.

Emergencies

Most of the debt we accrue is voluntary and unnecessary. However, unexpected crises frequently result in debt. Your financial situation can quickly alter as a result of a car accident, a serious medical emergency, a lawsuit, or a natural disaster.

When people don't have enough money set aside for emergencies, it's sometimes inevitable that they end up taking on massive sums of debt. This debt is just as harmful even though it is for a worthy cause. Additionally, given to the often enormous sums involved, it may be more difficult to recover from emergency debt.

Job Loss

Regular remuneration from work offers a lot of security and the assurance that there will be enough money to cover expenses and put food on the table.

You can have upcoming payments or be forced to use credit or debt companies to pay your expenses if you unexpectedly lose your job or are unable to pay your invoices.

In these situations, accessibility to savings or reliable insurance coverage can be helpful. If you are not able to preserve your funds, it is worth investigating whether you may be eligible for government assistance in the form of subsidies.

Student Debt

Last but not least is a concept you are probably well aware of. Even if you lucked out and don't carry any student debt of your own, you most definitely know someone who does. It has become one of the most common forms of debt among people in the United States and beyond.

This kind of painful debt is in fact extremely prevalent, particularly among young people like yourself. Attending college or continuing your education with a postgraduate program can be a big step toward assisting you reach your objectives and advance in your chosen field of work. Unfortunately, it is also very expensive to pursue both undergraduate and graduate degrees, particularly in the United States.

When you actually begin working, a small percentage of the debt will be deducted from your pay in a manner distinct from other types of debt.

The good news is that your credit score won't likely suffer if you have student loan debt, unlike certain other types of debt. But that is really the only break you are given when it comes to student debt.

Credit Cards & Debt

We need to take a good, hard look at credit cards. To be quite honest, credit cards get something of a bad reputation among people. Earlier in this book, you were informed that slicing up and destroying your credit cards might be a move that you have to make if you have a problem with spending. That is still true.

But you shouldn't completely count out and ignore credit cards if you can keep your spending in check. The reality is that credit cards *can* serve a purpose and can help you make ends meet, enjoy your life, and build your credit so that you can afford more and be given more opportunities in the future.

However, you need to understand the pros and cons of credit cards before you spend them. What should you do, how should you use them, and what should you avoid when you are using plastic over cash?

Credit Cards Dos And Don'ts

Now it is time to discuss another of the most popular products related to your personal finance: a credit card.

You are well aware of credit cards. They are everywhere and advertised all over the internet and television screens. But you need to really understand the intricate details of these handy and ubiquitous forms of payment. Once you understand credit cards better, you will be much safer with them.

And safety is the most important thing to know when you are using a credit card.

If you have never had a credit card before, or only heard of them, then you likely have a lot of questions about them. How do they work? Are they really that impactful on your financial standings and your future? Do you really need to get one? And, most importantly, how do you get one and use it correctly and safely?

See, there is a lot to learn about credit cards.

How Do Credit Cards Work?

A credit card that you get from a financial company is tied to a credit account that is in your name. Keep in mind that your credit account will be directly tied to your social security number, ensuring that it is really and truly linked to you. Therefore, no matter where you go and what you do, the credit account will be designated yours and impossible to part from. You can't wish a credit account away or avoid it.

When you are approved for a credit card, you can use it to buy just about anything. From groceries to computers to cars, clothing, and beyond, a credit card is as good as immediate cash. The thing is, there is no cash. It's all credit. It's essentially the credit card company paying for the goods you want. And then, by the agreed upon due date, you simply pay them back.

Makes sense, right?

The amount of money that you owe on a credit card is called your balance. If you buy something with your credit card that costs you $250 then your balance will have $250 added to it.

Now, you might think that you have no limits when it comes to your credit card. You can just go out there and spend, spend, spend as long as you pay the amount back to the company over time, right?

Wrong. You actually have something called a credit limit. The credit limit is the maximum amount that you can owe to the financial institution that approved your card at one time. If your credit limit is $500, you will not be able to go over that amount. A common credit limit, especially for new credit users, is around $1,000. If you spend $999, you are fine. If you try to spend $1,001, your credit card will be denied.

The margin between the credit limit you have and your balance is your "available credit." If your credit limit is $500 and you spend $400 with the card over a few months, your available credit will be $100. This is all very easy to keep tabs on and be aware of, especially with smartphone apps from your credit card company that will keep you up to date with your credit limit, available credit, and other important information.

How To Build Credit

As has been mentioned multiple times, you want to maintain a good credit score. And there are multiple ways to keep your score strong and build your credit for the future. Building your credit is a smart move because it will allow you to get cards with higher credit limits and more perks, and will improve your credit score so you can get different sorts of financing, approval for cards, apartments, homes, and more.

But how do you do it? There is more to it than you think and certain things you should keep in mind when you get your first credit card.

Pay On Time

Here is the best and smartest way to build your credit and keep your score intact and as high as possible.

To do this you need to pay off your credit card on time. It's as simple as that. Your payment history is a huge part of your credit score and just one missed payment can send you down a spiral that will soon have your score in the low 600s or 500s.

Your credit card company will make it incredibly easy to pay on time. They will let you know of your due date and the "minimum amount" that you have to pay. Of course, you can pay *more* than that amount if it's possible but you need to at least deposit the minimum amount to your credit card company.

It is best to pay early and pay often. It is smart to set up auto-pay so that your bank checking account automatically deposits the money owed to your credit card company.

Do whatever you have to to make sure that you are always paying on time, early, and to the full extent required to you by your credit card company. It doesn't matter how you remember to pay but you *must* stay on top of this or else your credit score will start to dwindle.

How To Pay Off Your Debt

Did you know that the average American has about $96,000 of debt, including their mortgages, credit cards, and student debt?

That's an awful lot of money. Have you ever even seen that much money at one time? Probably not. But that doesn't mean that you can't pay it off and get rid of it. Paying down even about $100,000 worth of debt is possible, if you know what to do and follow the steps laid out for you.

Make no mistake: paying off a lot of debt isn't easy. It takes time - a lot of time. And it takes dedication - lots of that too. But it will be well worth it. If you stick with your plan and make some changes to your life, you will be debt free and able to enjoy your life without the weight of debt on your shoulders.

Debt Snowball

Perhaps the most common, and smartest approach to eliminating and handling your debt is something called the "debt snowball". It is easy to understand and makes perfect sense. In fact, it makes the task of getting rid of your debt seem actually attainable and not too challenging, as long as you follow the plan.

As you begin to pay back creditors, the debt snowball strategy gathers steam, similar to a rolling snowball over the snow. Pay off your obligations starting with the lesser ones first. List your debts in order of balance, starting with the smallest. As long as the debt with the tiniest balance isn't paid in full, make sure to pay the minimum on all other bills and additional money to that one.

Apply the same plan to any additional debts. As you settle bills, you'll have more money to pay down other loans. Additionally, making progress is motivating and can help you stay on pace for debt repayment.

Debt Avalanche

Since there is a debt snowfall approach, there is obviously a debt avalanche strategy too. With this approach, you should arrange all of your debts according to their rates. You should first list all of your loans in order of highest to lowest interest rate. After that, while committing to the minimum payments on all other loans, you focus on repaying the debt with the highest interest rate foremost. As a result, you pay less in interest and have more money available to pay down other debt.

Debt Consolidation

Through debt consolidation, individuals can pay off all of their debts with a single loan and a single monthly payment.

Additionally, consolidation may result in a cheaper interest rate and provide an opportunity to work out a better repayment schedule for some debts.

Through debt consolidation, the creditor settles all of your outstanding bills and combines them into a single loan. Even though the revised interest rate could be greater compared to some of the existing payments, by eliminating missed and late payment fines, you can ultimately save money.

You must compute your composite interest rate in order to ascertain whether it is a wise course of action for your circumstances. It represents the total interest rate on all of your debts. It is computed by adding up all of the annual interest payments and dividing them by the total amount owing.

Although the interest rate on a loan for debt consolidation can be pretty high, it may still be less expensive than the combined rate you are currently paying. In that case it would be a wise decision to take out a debt consolidation loan.

If you can promise that you won't use your credit cards or take on further debt as you try to pay off what you owe, you might want to think about debt consolidation.

Debt Management

Most nonprofit credit counseling organizations can assist individuals in creating a debt management strategy. A company will speak with the businesses you owe the money to and seek reductions on your account. This can require negotiating reduced payments, creating fair repayment schedules, or potentially obtaining debt relief.

If you have difficulty making your minimal monthly payments and would rather have a plan that will help you pay very little in interest and pay off your debt more quickly, debt consolidation may be a good alternative for you.

Why You NEED To Get Rid Of Your Debt

There are actually many reasons why you should get rid of debt as quickly as you can. There are few things that keep you tethered and tied to the present more than debt. You will not be able to build a strong, true future with financial freedom if debt is holding you down.

Aside from just being free of it, what are the biggest most common reasons why you should eliminate your debt?

Debt Holds You Back

The simple and sad truth is that you aren't going anywhere if you still have a bunch of debt piled up on you.

We all have big plans with our lives. We want a steady job, a nice place to live, and the ability to truly enjoy ourselves when we want. But we cannot do that unless we get our debt under control. You have to think of debt as a big, heavy weight tied around you. You can *try* to do other things, and you might actually accomplish them. But it will be a whole lot harder when the debt is still tied to you.

Debt prevents you from achieving the most with your money, which poses a severe risk to your ability to maintain financial stability. What you put toward debt repayments might be set aside for your retirement, or the college education of your children, or a new home, car, or other high-profile item. You'll have more room in your budget to work toward financial security after you're debt-free.

When you borrow in order to pay for stuff, you have less cash available for the activities you actually want to do in life.

Sadly, this causes many people to become even more indebted. They are unable to make purchases due to their debt, so they keep borrowing to do so and then eventually they run out of borrowing options. This pattern of debt repayment is broken, allowing you to use your money to purchase the things you truly value.

It Adds So Much Stress

There are enough things in your life that cause stress. Sometimes it's your job, sometimes it's interpersonal relationships, sometimes it's traffic. The bottom line is that life throws a lot at you and that can add to your stress levels rather quickly.

There is no doubt that debt will only add more. When you have a lot of debt, you always have something more to worry about. Even if you have a great day and accomplish everything you want, the debt is still waiting for you. Until you are free from it, it is always looming over you and that will make you feel stressed out and uncomfortable and generally very unhappy.

Debt might cause additional stress since you are concerned about how you'll pay off all the debt as well as other expenditures. While occasional stress is harmless, chronic stress can cause major health problems up to and including even heart attacks. In rare circumstances, getting out of debt can genuinely save your life.

You have a little more debt to manage and pay off as there are more individuals you owe money to. You'll receive fewer bills in the mail each month once you're debt-free. There won't be many monthly bills for you to be concerned about, such as electricity, healthcare, and phone service, all of which don't require minimum payments, accrued interest, or lengthy commitments.

Your Credit Score Is Hurt

If you want to get approved for an apartment, a home, a new car, or even the best new cell phone on the market, you need to have a credit score that isn't down in the dumps.

When people spend wildly and ruin their credit by accumulating debt, they are not able to have many of the great things that we all desire. And that is the main reason why you should eliminate your debt to keep your credit rating strong. If you don't do this, then it could take years upon years to really improve your score, get in healthy shape, and be able to do the things that you want.

Your credit score may suffer if you have excessive debt, particularly credit card debt. Your credit score suffers when you have significant credit card balances in relation to your credit limit. The same holds true if your balances are substantial compared to the total borrowed. Another advantage of being debt-free is that it improves your credit rating.

It's preferable to set an example whenever it comes to money. Tell them the value of being debt-free and demonstrate it by living a debt-free life for them if you want your kids to avoid debt. Your financial lessons will appear less hypocritical in this manner.

You are only stealing from your future income when you obtain a loan or use your credit card. Therefore, whether you spend $100 or $20,000 now, it will be deducted from your future earnings. When you remember this, you will likely work hard to not pull out a lot of money and go further into debt. It might feel good to spend that money now but you will most definitely regret it in the future.

Having debt lowers your future level of living since it leaves you with less money than you do now. So, if you want a bright future with many possibilities and options and a life that you can truly enjoy, free of stress, you should be doing all that you can to maintain, manage, and get rid of all debt.

What About Student Debt?

Since you are young and possibly in school, the chances of you having student debts are probably quite high. Nowadays, nearly everyone who attends an institute of higher learning will gain this sort of debt. It is sadly the price of doing business.

Yes, going to college is a business and that means it requires pay - lots of it. In order to pay for tuition, people will take out thousands of dollars in student loans, with the goal of paying them back in time. How much time? Well, that depends on what sort of repayment plan you agree to.

The scary reality is that student loan debt can be massive. It will quickly balloon to a number that no one is comfortable with. But it is something you have to live with.

But you don't have to live with it forever.

Paying off your student loan debt is achievable, and you can do it faster than ever if you follow a few smart tips, work hard, and stay dedicated to the plan that you create.

Make Extra Payments

This step is obviously one of the smartest if you want to pay off your student loan debt as quickly as possible. Of course, it is easier said than done. But if you are able to do so, making extra payments is a great way to whittle down the amount you owe.

Yes, it is true that if you want to manage your student debt really well, you should attempt to make greater payments to pay down the principal more rapidly and shorten the duration of the loan. You can shorten the loan term and the amount of interest paid by lowering the principal sum.

For instance, a financial aid loan with a $30,000 balance and an approximate 7% interest rate would require monthly payments of at least $300. You can see from an online loan calculator that paying $400 per month rather than $300 per month will allow the borrower to pay off the loan in fewer than seven years.

Paying every two weeks rather than monthly is another tactic. Of course, all of this will only be possible if you have a good source of income coming in, which leads us to our next tip.

Get A Job

You have a lot on your plate when you're a student and you might not have the time for it but getting a job, even a part-time one, can really help you secure the funds needed to take care of your student loan debt faster than most people. Every dollar that you can funnel into paying off your debt is a dollar that you will have later in life.

Having a job when in school can help you manage your student debt since you can use the money you make to lower the amount you borrow initially and turn your repayment plan even simpler. Earning up to $7,040 annually won't have an impact on your ability to get additional financial aid.

To find out whether there are any campus job openings, consult the information or career center at school. Employment on campus is typically more accommodating of odd or hectic school schedules. There are even more online jobs available than ever, offering you additional opportunities that fit your schedule and skill set. You can work full-time summer employment between those school years to increase your income.

Refinance

By securing a reduced interest rate, a smaller payment period, or both, restructuring or refinancing your student loans may enable you to pay them off more quickly.

Be aware that if you haven't managed to establish a strong credit score or you have a bankable co-signer, this option might not be accessible straight away after you graduate. If not, building your credit history and being eligible for refinance lenders may take a while. You must also have a history of consistent employment or income in order to qualify with many lenders.

Refinancing federal student loans will prevent you from taking advantage of some advantages, such as income-driven repayment plans and student debt forgiveness programs.

You should take a look at several lenders prior to any refinancing to determine who provides you the greatest deals. A student debt refinance calculator will help you comprehend the numbers and decide whether this is the best course of action.

Talk To Your Employer

Several loan firms now provide tuition reimbursement or help with repaying student loans. For employees that enroll in degree programs inside a predetermined network of courses and schools, some firms, like Starbucks and Walmart, even provide free tuition.

Through 2025, employers may potentially contribute $5,250 yearly toward a worker's college expenses or help with student loan repayment. This bonus is not taxable for the worker, which is obviously a huge benefit for those who are working and going to school at the same time.

Everybody wins since employers can also write off the cost. To find out what options your firm offers for student debt repayment or tuition help, consult your employee handbook or contact the HR department.

How Long Should Your Student Loan Debt Last?

Based on the interest rates, outstanding balance, annual income, and repayment plan for your loans, it normally takes approximately 10 to 30 years to clear your student loan debt.

The length of time it takes you to pay off your student loans is significantly influenced by the repayment strategy you choose. Although prolonged and progressive repayment plans for government loans with terms of 25 to 30 years are also an option, they are not as common as the normal 10-year repayment period for student loans.

You can pay around 10 and 20 percent of your expendable income for 20 to 25 years under income-driven repayment arrangements. The remaining balance is then canceled.

When a student owns private loans, they may typically choose a repayment period that suits you: anywhere between five and twenty years. Refinancing your private loans if you require extra time is always a smart idea.

You need to look at your money, your obligations, and the outstanding debt that hangs over your head. This is something you can start today and it will be the first step to moving forward, wrapping your arms around the debt, and beginning to eliminate it too.

There is no need to wait. If you have debt, you need to start controlling and minimizing it. That is something that can start right now, this very day.

Next Steps

Before you can cancel any debt and get a handle on the money that you might owe, you need to know just where things stand.

Therefore, the first thing you should do as soon as possible is have an honest look at the money that you owe. You can do this today and knowing the lay of the land when it comes to your finances is *key* to making things right.

Pull out your financial documents, especially those related to credit cards and student loans. By going through all of these, you will have a concrete number of the money you owe and the debt you have.

You need to look at your money, your obligations, and the outstanding debt that hangs over your head. This is something you can start today and it will be the first step to moving forward, wrapping your arms around the debt, and beginning to eliminate it too.

There is no need to wait. If you have debt, you need to start controlling and minimizing it. That is something that can start right now, this very day.

Step 4:
Insurance

If you are a young person lucky enough to own a car then you surely know a thing or two about the basic concept behind insurance.

When you buy into an insurance plan, you are essentially covering your bases if a bad accident ever arises. If your car gets ruined at any point, the insurance company that you pay monthly will be able to get your car back in working shape, or perhaps even provide you with a new one if the damage is too much.

Insurance is literally mandatory if you are driving a car but insurance plans outside of automobile ones are *not*. There are many people who don't ever look into getting a life insurance policy because they don't think it's needed.

And the people who *do* buy life insurance are hardly ever young. Yet, younger people should really pay attention to all the benefits that life insurance can bring them. It might not seem like it but it's money well spent.

There are multiple types of insurance and multiple reasons why you should buy into them when you are young. You shouldn't be waiting for old age and fatigue and the wear and tear of life to strike. You should be proactive, look out for yourself and your future, and invest in insurance when you are still young and there is so much life left ahead of you.

Let's start with a discussion of life insurance. At a young age, the idea of buying a life insurance policy seems downright preposterous but there are many reasons why you should look into it when you are still young. Let's take a look at a few of them.

Why You Should Get Life Insurance When You're Young

While you are now still youthful and lacking any care in the world, as you become older, your obligations will increase. Today, you are probably solely worried about going to work, staying close to friends and family, and living the sort of life that you want to.

But that won't be the case in the years ahead. As college and schooling is placed in the rearview mirror, your mind and life will be consumed with other things that seem much more adult and mature.

If you have kids, you'll need to save money for their schooling, as well as your retirement, taking care of your elderly parents, and more.

What amount will you be able to put aside for the welfare of the family if you wait until a later age to begin making plans for all of this, taking rising prices and the uncertain economic conditions and the unforeseen speed bumps of life into consideration? If you don't plan ahead and plan well, you are only setting yourself up for disaster.

This is when life insurance is useful.

The adage "age is just a number" is well known. Nevertheless, when viewed through the perspective of life insurance, age is the main element that affects how costly or affordable your coverage will be. If you pay a large premium or a low one is dependent on the age when you obtain a life insurance policy.

Life Insurance Favors The Young

With a good life insurance plan, you are ensuring that your friends and family will be able to be comfortable after your passing. A life insurance policy divides your assets up and sends them to several people, all of your choosing.

If you really want to look out for the people you care about most, you need a life insurance policy and you really should look into getting one when you are still young.

And your young age benefits you in so many ways when you are younger. That is because health is the key to lower insurance rates. A 20-year-old has better health than somebody double that age, thus they have to pay less for insurance. Since their young life and chosen profession is still progressing, the income growth will keep the rates even more reasonable. It is crucial to remember that the premium doesn't really change with age throughout the duration of the insurance and remains the same.

Think about the following instance: A 25-year-old person as well as a 45-year-old buy a term policy with an amount assured of $1,00,00,000 that is valid for forty years. The yearly premium for the youthful individual would only be $5,000 for forty years, as opposed to the older person's $11,200 for 20 years.

The 20-year-old gets insured for twice as long a time but only pays 50% of the entire price. While the 40-year-old pays more than twice as much in total premium, they are only protected for half as long as the 20-year-old.

Youngsters would have less money saved up, particularly at the beginning of their careers. Yet, they likely have the most obligations and dependencies. These could include elderly parents, young brothers and sisters who need to go to school, or perhaps even relatives who are suffering from serious illnesses. Also possible are unpaid bills or a significant upcoming family event, like a wedding or the birth of a new child. There is an unbalanced distribution of earning members to dependents.

Younger people are much less likely to have substantial funds to cover any unexpected financial need brought on by their illness, incapacity, or death. As a result, the greatest way to safeguard their family's financial security is through insurance. This is a crucial factor to take into account when purchasing risk coverage. Keep in mind that the cheaper premiums are advantageous the earlier you purchase. The future of your family will be safeguarded by insurance in the event of any unforeseen circumstances.

In a similar vein, life insurance can make it easier to plan out routine savings and designate them for particular requirements. This will assist you in covering both critical and impulsive expenses as well as planned and unanticipated ones. Why does this matter? How about using preparing for your child's education as an illustration. Savings-linked insurance plans, for example, will ensure that mandatory savings are made for the designated requirement and are locked in until maturity.

The ability to create a corpus, either by oneself or by the insurance provider, in the event of an emergency brought on by a death, disability, or disease is its most significant feature. Additionally, the tight structure of the insurance policy will prevent the money being saved for the child's education from being spent on something that would later cause regret.

These characteristics, advantages, and rewards make purchasing life insurance for an individual in their 20s a worthwhile option.

Your insurance policy selection must take into account your long-term objectives and needs.

Plan for the Long Term

Term insurance is one of the most common and proven forms of life insurance that you should be thinking of buying into.

This kind of insurance is the simplest and least expensive. In the tragic event of an accident, sickness, or death due to natural causes, term insurance is a pure risk plan that's also purchased to safeguard your future wages and the financial security of your family. Since it protects your life for a certain period of time, typically between 10 and 40 years, it is known as a term plan. The policy ends after that time period.

The set premiums of this type of policy must be paid throughout the duration of the premium-paying term in order to maintain the policy's validity. The principal amount is paid to the beneficiary as a death benefit if the policyholder passes away prior to the policy term expiring. But there is no compensation if the insured person lives past the specified time.

Even more protection against severe diseases and accidents is provided by some term insurance policies, making it even more appealing.

Lifelong Planning

Anyone who is up to the age of 99 is covered by whole life insurance.

The main distinction between whole life and term insurance is that whole life plans offer a guaranteed payout because they protect a person up to 99 years old.

These plans offer three types of benefits: death, survival, and maturity. But, the premium for these plans can be nearly three times as much as a term plan. Both regular and fixed-term premium payment choices cover the policyholders for the duration of their lives.

Insurance Strategy with Units (ULIPs)

Your obligations change as you age, there is no denying that.

Taking care of elderly parents, funding a child's education, and purchasing a home are a few of these. With its combined benefits of investment and insurance, ULIP offers tailored solutions that can change to meet your requirements and preferences. A yearly or monthly premium payment is made, with a portion going toward the insurance coverage and the remainder put into stocks, bonds, or a mixture of the both.

Although ULIPs have the potential to be excellent wealth creators, because the returns are market-linked, they are susceptible to market risks. But the ability to move funds easily and the choice of a partial withdrawal can help to mitigate this. When the insured person dies, the life insurance is paid to the beneficiaries; if the insured person survives the policy period, the policy pays the maturity amount.

Plan of Endowment

Endowment provides both insurance and savings, which is a double advantage. It encourages consistent saving over a predetermined time period with a minimal guarantee of cash assured paid at maturity. Building a corpus for needs like your retirement or children's education through endowment is a wonderful idea.

The maturity amount is compensated if the insured lives through the policy's expiration date. The beneficiaries will get the sum guaranteed as well as a bonus, if appropriate, in the tragic event of the insured's early death. As a result, endowment is a strategy with no risk and a set level of return guarantees.

Retirement strategy

Do you believe you are not young enough to consider retirement? Consider the savings on your premium and the significant growth of your corpus. As a result, you will have a good 30-35 years to accumulate wealth, and because of the compounding impact, your returns will be higher.

Retirement programs provide both investing and insurance benefits. The premiums may be paid systematically and on schedule, sometimes known as pension schemes. Retirement insurance includes whole life insurance with recurring payouts after a specific time. Single premium immediate annuity products ensure a steady stream of income during your retirement years.

Health Insurance At A Young Age

Buying Health Insurance When You're Young

When you are younger, healthy, and rarely visit the doctor, bypassing a health insurance plan may appear to be a good way to save cash in the near term.

Sudden diseases and accidents do, regrettably, occur, and they are significantly more costly if you don't have insurance.

Without insurance, the average cost of anything like a leg injury from snowboarding, biking, or participating in sports is more than $7,000. And even a short stay in the hospital may reach around $25,000 in total.

It's in fact advantageous to pay a little monthly premium for a healthcare plan that prevents you from having to pay for unforeseen medical expenses out of your pocket, particularly these days when health insurance is more reasonably priced than ever. Plans for $10 or less are available for a number of people, especially younger folks who are typically fairly healthy.

The great news is that although health insurance requires an initial commitment, it caps your annual outlay for medical care. For instance, hospitalization coverage is one of the advantages that health plans that have received ACA approval must by law include. This indicates that having health insurance, whether or not you usually use it, helps shield you from insolvency in case of a medical emergency.

Feeling good? Buying a health insurance plan is a great way to keep that the truth. Regular physicals, vaccinations, and cancer screenings are a few examples of the health services that can help you identify illnesses before they become serious, keeping you healthy as you age. Preventive care is what we call this.

Each health plan includes free preventative treatment that can keep you healthy and young and many of them come without even a copay. You could purchase the most affordable health insurance and still have the ability to enjoy annual physicals, visits related to female health including pap smears, vaccinations, blood pressure and cholesterol checks, and a lot more by purchasing even more affordable plans, which include all the preventive care services as other more expensive options.

You might be eligible for a subsidy, or funds that the government will contribute to your monthly premiums, based upon your yearly income. Nearly half of all Americans today actually have access to these subsidies, which can significantly lower the cost of health insurance. Certain people's plans even result in a loss of money.

You'll note when looking for health insurance that various plans are divided into four "metallic" tiers: bronze, silver, gold, and platinum. Price and degree of coverage rise with each metal tier.

The costliest policies, platinum ones, will definitely cover the majority of your medical expenses.

Choose a bronze plan if you will not need medical attention frequently to save money. Bronze plans typically have higher deductibles, so you'll have to pay more out of pocket if you do require medical attention. These plans, however, cap your yearly medical expenses, safeguarding you in the event of a medical emergency without demanding significant monthly payments.

Additionally, bronze plans completely cover preventative care, so you can continue to receive your yearly exam and other services at no cost.

You might also think about a catastrophic plan if you're under 30 and don't anticipate needing a lot of medical attention. Don't be alarmed by the word; this kind of health insurance is merely a more affordable choice for younger individuals.

Because catastrophic plans feature extremely high deductibles in exchange for cheap monthly premiums, their main objective is to safeguard your finances in the event of a medical emergency. Unlike other insurance policies, catastrophic plans also include three annual visits to a primary care physician.

How To Get Health Insurance When You're Young

Get It From Your Parents

Your parent's health insurance policy may cover you. Young adults can continue to be covered by their parents' health insurance until they are 26 thanks to the Affordable Care Act.

Prior to the ACA, insurance providers had the right to drop registered children as early as age 19, and occasionally as late as age 30 for full-time students. Today, the majority of children's health insurance plans are required to offer coverage to youngsters until the age of 26.

The legislation simplifies the process and makes it far more economical for young individuals to obtain health insurance coverage by permitting you to continue on a parent's plan. Even if you're married, residing away at school, not enrolled full-time, financially secure, or qualified to participate in an employer's plan, you can enlist or stay on your parents' policy.

Affordable Insurance Exchanges

Health insurance may now be purchased more easily and affordably thanks to what are called "affordable insurance exchanges".

These exchanges permit individuals and small companies to evaluate health plans, get solutions to inquiries, discover if they are entitled to tax credits for private health insurance and register a health plan that matches their requirements.

An exchange can assist you in finding and comparing private health insurance policies, receiving clarification on your available alternatives, determining your eligibility for health programs and government-run credits that lower the cost of coverage, and enrolling in a plan that best suits your requirements.

The exchange serves as a single location for both individuals and families to sign up for private or government-sponsored health insurance.

Medicaid

Medicaid is a government-run and funded health insurance program that is accessible to a select group of individuals, including low-income families and disabled individuals.

The requirements for Medicaid enrollment differ from state to state, but generally speaking, only individuals who are not qualified for another sort of health insurance and who meet the necessary level of poverty are entitled for Medicaid coverage.

Individual Policies

You can get insurance on your own. According to the ACA, health insurance policies cannot restrict or refuse coverage for a child under the age of 19 due to a "pre-existing condition", which is a medical condition that existed when the child applied to enroll in the plan. These safeguards are now available to all Americans thanks to the ACA.

COBRA

This program permits you to buy the health plan your parents now have for you in order to maintain coverage once your coverage under their plan ends. The length of the coverage is up to 36 months.

Your folks ought to get in touch with their company's human resources department, benefits manager, or local Department of Labor for more information on COBRA insurance and your benefits under COBRA law.

Why You Should Buy Health Insurance - Even Though You're Young

There really are so many reasons why you should look to buy health insurance, even though you are currently young and don't have a care in the world when it comes to your own personal well-being.

The biggest reason that you should get health insurance as soon as possible is because you never know what's about to happen. You don't know what sort of fate awaits you, what sort of accidents or mishaps might be right around the corner, and when you might need to be seen by a doctor.

It might be a bad illness you didn't see coming, an accident completely out of your control, or just you being young and a bit careless but there are many catalysts for needing to visit a medical professional. And chances are you cannot handle the costs of doing that completely on your own.

Paying out of pocket for the doctor is always a pain in the neck but it's especially bad when you are young and are not making the sort of money a professional who has been employed for decades might have.

The other reason you should be getting health insurance right now is because it's never been easier and so inexpensive to do so. Because of the creation of the Affordable Care Act, health insurance is accessible to just about any type of American.

The government will actually *help* you get your health insurance, via their website and the subsidies they will provide you with. They *want* you to get a plan and will actually charge you if you don't. It doesn't matter how much you make or what job you have or what sort of plan you need, something is easily found via the government and the ACA.

But perhaps the biggest reason why you should be buying health insurance, even though you're young, is because doing so is a very smart financial choice to make.

Experiencing a medical emergency or serious medical issue can be one of the worst things to happen to your bank account. In fact, there are millions of people who actually declare bankruptcy because of the financial strain that paying medical bills puts on them. There is no faster way to accumulate a mountain of debt than a medical emergency.

With a good insurance plan, you can avoid running into money problems that will be with you for years. Like student loan debt, the debt incurred because of situations like this can be long-lasting and can remain on your record and weigh you down for decades.

Who wants to enter their adult lives with this nagging problem hanging over their heads? Not many, and a health insurance plan can do away with these problems, if not entirely at least partially.

There are multiple reasons why you should be getting insurance for yourself when you're still young and in the prime of your life.

You have learned a lot about multiple types of insurance and now it's your task to find the plans that are right for you. It's not just about keeping you healthy and looking out for the well-being of those you love the most, it's about saving yourself money and being smart with your finances, now and far in the future.

Next Steps

Insurance might sometimes be a pain and finding the right policy for you requires a lot of work and that is why your first step is to start researching what sort of insurance you want and how much it will cost you.

Since you are young, you have a few options. You can look through the government's website, you can inquire with your parents about their plans, or you can try to create a plan of your own.

The first step for you should be researching and, luckily for you, there is plenty of that to be done.

You can even start by simply Googling ideal insurance plans for someone your age. This will be the start of you reading, taking notes, budgeting, and figuring which insurance policy is right for you.

Step 5:
Investing Your Money

"The biggest risk of all is not taking one."
— *Mellody Hobson*

If you really want to make each and every buck you have stretch far and accomplish a lot, investing it is a very smart move.

There aren't many young people who invest their money. Whether it be the stock market, a retirement plan, cryptocurrency, or something else, people who haven't lived much life don't often see the appeal of putting their money into investments.

Why is that? Well, for one, it is very complicated. Investing isn't an easy thing to figure out and it's even harder to master. There is a lot to learn, a lot to keep in mind, and a very steep learning curve.

Also, young people usually want a fast return on investment. If they are putting their money into something with the hopes of making more, they want that extra cash as soon as possible. It's not really all that fun to sit and slowly watch an investment grow over weeks, months, or even years.

But if you are trying to get a good handle on your personal finance, especially at a young age, then you should study the world of investing and find the right way to make your money count even more. Now more than ever, there are many ways for you to invest. Even if you haven't done anything like this before, you shouldn't be afraid and you shouldn't avoid investing. It's one of the best ways to make one dollar turn into two or three or four or more.

What Is Investing?

Purchasing assets which gain value through time and offer returns in the shape of income checks or capital gains is the practice of investing.

In a broader sense, investment can also mean devoting time or resources to bettering your own or others' lives. But in the realm of finance, investing refers to the act of buying stocks, real estate, and other things of value with the intention of making money or capital gains.

The simplest way to understand how investing works is to acquire an item (like a stock or commodity) for a cheap cost and then sell it for a better, higher price. This type of investment return is referred to as a capital gain. One strategy to make money investing is to generate returns by achieving capital gains or selling assets for a profit.

So, you know what investing is but what are the best ways for a younger person like yourself to invest your money and make your finances blossom and grow even more?

Invest In A 401(k)

If you are working for a company, you might be able to invest your money in your very own retirement fund. As mentioned before, it's never too early to begin thinking about your retirement, even though you might be young and just starting out in your career.

Thankfully, many companies are willing to offer you a 401(k). But even if your place of business is giving this to you because of your commitment to them, you can still put more money into it. In fact, investing in your 401(k) is a rather brilliant move.

The best part about investing in your 401(k) is that your company might match the contribution that you make. If your company offers a match, then it will deposit the same amount that you contribute to your 401(k), up to a certain percent.

So if the place you work for says it'll give you a 5% match on any contribution, it will put 5% of your investment into your 401(k). So, why wouldn't you want to invest your $1,000 into your 401(k)? Imagine how much money your company would match when you do that.

A 401(k) is a retirement fund that will be waiting for you when you are no longer working. However, unlike an IRA, a 401(k) will be offered to you from your place of work and will often be matched by them as well.

If you are thinking of investing, you should check in with HR for your work. They will give you pointers and tell you the proper steps to follow to smartly invest your money in your account and make sure that it'll be there waiting for you when you finally reach retirement age.

The thing about a 401(k) is that it can truly change your life and make your twilight years enjoyable, fun, and stress free. But so many people aren't even aware that they have one. You might be getting important information about your 401(k) in the mail and it might just be sitting in an anonymous envelope from your employer. That is why you should talk to your HR department if you are thinking of putting your money into your 401(k).

Play The Stock Market

Investing in the stock market is not always easy and it certainly comes with many challenges and stresses. Additionally, it has a steep learning curve so you will really want to study hard if you choose to go down this route.

But playing the stock market is one of the best ways to invest. It has always been attractive, even to those who have never invested before in their lives.

There are many ways to invest and many benefits to each type of investor. You can simply research the market, find a stock that you like, invest your money and then walk away and let the market rise, fall, and just do what it does.

You can also become a day trader, someone who puts their money into a stock in the morning and then moves it around by the end of the same day. This requires a lot more attention to detail, a lot more work too, but you can cobble together a big, sizable amount of cash in a short amount of time.

The stock market has provided a lot of money for a lot of people for a lot of years. And the best part about investing your money this way is that there is plenty to read about investing and many methods, tricks, and pointers that you can pick up from proven investors who have made a pretty penny over the years.

From Apple to Walmart, Berkshire Hathaway, Citi Bank, Google, Amazon, and beyond, there are just so many stocks that you can put your hard-earned money into. An entire world awaits anyone who wants to try out the stock market to see their investment grow and flourish on Wall Street.

Get Into Cryptocurrencies

Cryptocurrencies are a rather new sensation but it has paid out a lot for many investors over the last few years.

Have you heard of Bitcoin? Of course you have, it has been in the news so much lately. But you might not know how it works and the minute details about it and the rest of the cryptocurrencies out there. But the bottom line is this:

cryptocurrencies are a form of digital currencies that can be used for so many goods and services. The only thing about crypto is that you never physically hold it in your hands, it is always only online.

There are over 3,000 cryptocurrencies in existence, which means you have a lot to choose from. But there are many online forums, books, and newsletters that you can sign up for. Just browsing them will give you some pointers and have you headed in the right direction when it comes to investing.

You need to be aware of one major thing: the cryptocurrency market is very volatile. It's not uncommon for crypto to lose a lot of value in a short amount of time. You should expect many ups and downs when you are investing in crypto. But you should also be prepared for a sizable return on your investment.

Which cryptocurrency do you want to put your cash into? Which one is the most exciting? Which one seems like the next big thing? That is for you to decide. It's a tricky, complicated, and, yes, risky investment but it could pay out very well for you.

It is important that when you are investing in cryptocurrency you remember a few things, beyond the volatility of the marketplace. Firstly, there are many different cryptos, or coins, you can put your money into. You don't have to invest all that much in just one choice. You can actually put your money into many different coins. There are many coins that cost less than a dollar to invest. Spread the wealth around if you have faith in the cryptos you find.

You should also spend time researching cryptocurrency before you actually put your money where your mouth is. Don't rush! Spend your time learning all you need to know and read, read, read a lot so you know what you're talking about and what you're doing.

There is a lot to learn about cryptocurrency and it can be a great way for you to turn your money into a whole lot more. But do not enter this marketplace without studying it thoroughly first.

Peer-To-Peer Lending

Maybe you want to take your money and put it into a business or idea that you think can pay off and become the next big thing. If that is the case, then peer-to-peer lending is one of the best ways to invest. In just a short amount of time, you can take your money and offer it to those who need it and then watch a cause or business you believe bloom, blossom, and flourish into so much more.

What is peer-to-peer lending? It is a way for you to give small amounts of your own money, or capital, to businesses and people that are trying to start companies or pursue a dream. And what do you get for investing your cash? Well, you will get an interest rate on your return. It sounds like a great way to invest your money because if you really are smart about your investing and find something that really does take off, you can make an awful lot of money.

The thing about peer-to-peer investing is that you have many ways to do it. From Lending Club to Prosper and other up-

and-coming platforms, you can invest today and quickly see the return on your investment grow.

At the same time, you should really make sure you are measured and smart when you take this approach to investing. This is business, after all, and you don't want to rush into anything. You should weigh both the pros and the cons about your possible investment and consider everything about it.

Is the marketplace right for the company you are investing in? Does it have room to grow? Do people really need the services it provides? There are all things you should take into consideration when you are starting your peer-to-peer lending career.

There is a growing number of companies, both small and large, who are turning to peer-to-peer lending to gain capital and find a way to thrive. It has never been a better time for you to contemplate putting your money into this form of investing. But there are risks and they need to be considered.

If you have ever wanted to invest in a company but have never really known how, then peer-to-peer lending is a great choice for you. For just several hundred dollars, you can find a company that needs your money, become an investor, and watch them turn into something substantial, successful, and good for your bottom line along with their own.

Use A Robo-Advisor

The stock market and investing in stocks isn't easy, and it's not for everyone. In fact, there are many people who don't even venture into the stock market because they are so scared and overwhelmed by the prospect of it and the particulars you have to learn.

There is no shame in admitting that you don't want to spend all the time and energy needed to learn about Wall Street or any trading market. However, you don't have to sit out on what could be a great investment just because you're feeling daunted by all the time you would spend learning the ins and outs of investing.

A robo-advisor is a great approach to investing if you want to be a part of the stock market but don't want to be sitting constantly at your computer, watching the market, and preparing to hit the right button at the right moment.

A robo-advisor just makes perfect sense for the modern day and age. It is an online service that uses automation for many parts of a financial plan that people used to have to do by hand. By using a robo-advisor, you can set the perimeters for your investment like when you want to buy shares, when you want to sell them, and more.

Then, after you have set up your robo-advisor you can sit back and just let it do all the work for you. Like the well-made, well-trained computer system it is, a robo-advisor will do everything for you and for only a small fee.

With automation involved, many of the fears that you have about buying stocks will be gone because you won't have to be sitting at your computer getting prepared to pull the trigger at the right time.

Robo-advisors do even more than just though, though. They can even choose the right shares for you, based upon your interests, the amount of your investment, and more. And the management fees related to robo-advisors are pretty agreeable.

At the end of the day, the thing that is best about a robo-advisor is that it takes out all the pain of setting up your portfolio, running it, and exercises any trades and sales and movements that you want. It's the ultimate evolution of the modern day stock market and it uses technology to get the job done, free of the stress and anxiety that usually comes with investing.

What To Keep In Mind When Investing

Know Why You Are Investing

No two investments are the same and you should always consider why you are investing when you are putting your money into any sort of stock, commodity, or product.

Whatever you invest for will determine how you invest. In order to assist your folks in paying down the mortgage on the home, you could be making investments. You may wish to invest money now so you have it when you reach retirement decades from now. Or maybe you just love the thrill of putting money into something and see it appreciate in value.

Each one of these investments has a completely distinct time frame and unique features that should be kept in mind at all times. Investors with shorter time horizons and want a pay out soon should work one way while those willing to ride it out for much longer will have another.

You should have a goal in mind when you begin investing and that goal will help you figure out just how cautious or risky you can be with your money.

Don't Forget The Risk

You must first determine your own risk tolerance prior to determining where and how and what to invest in. "Risk tolerance" is a technical term for the percentage of your investment that you are able to actually risk losing. You have an extremely low risk tolerance if you require cash to pay the rent for the following month. Meanwhile, your risk tolerance is extremely high if wasting your money entirely instead of investing would have no substantial impact on your life.

There are many risks when you are investing in something, because the market can change seemingly overnight without any warning, toying with your money and the amount of profit you are earning.

This is especially true for something like cryptocurrency because the market there is very volatile and has serious ups and downs in the span of just a few days. You need to be aware of this because investing with the belief that you will definitely make a lot of money, without exception, is a big mistake and will only lead to heartbreak and disappointment.

Don't forget to keep your "time horizon" in mind, which refers to the amount of time you plan to hold a certain investment. This will be a key factor in determining your risk tolerance.

Think About The Long Term

When investing your money, you should always be thinking of not next week but next year and the years ahead after that.

Numerous studies show that buyers who retain stocks and investments for longer than a decade will be compensated with greater yields that counterbalance some more immediate risks. However, risk never goes away, although you could argue it gets softer with time.

Diversification of your portfolio is essential no matter how long you want to invest. Another thing that is certain is that investing over a long period of time allows you to take advantage of the benefits of compounding. This is the method through which the money you earn gradually accrues interest. The benefits of compounding over time increase with the earlier you begin investing.

Stick To Your Plan

The fact that many investors sell their investments at the incorrect moment is one of the main causes of their bad returns. They frequently make choices based on current standings of the market and the world as it is right now. They consider what has lately performed well or poorly.

Some investors have a propensity to purchase items whose worth has increased and to sell items whose value has decreased. They don't put much thought into these things and really follow knee-jerk reactions they have.

Instead of doing this, you should develop a plan that you believe will enable you to achieve your objectives over the time you have available. Don't give up investing due to poor results. Follow your plan without purchasing or selling depending on your predictions of what may occur soon.

Investing has never been easier, especially in this day and age.

By putting your money in the right places, you can make even a modest amount become so much larger. It might not happen overnight; it might take time and it might be frustrating at times. But investing is a long game that takes time and pays off very well, if you know what you are doing.

Today, you can open up an account with Ameritrade, Robinhood, Merrill Lynch, or any other number of companies that will help take your money and put it exactly where you want. All you need is a plan.

Your next steps should be this: take a look at the world of investing and think of which commodity or stock sounds the most exciting for you. Maybe you're into cryptocurrency, maybe you want to put all your money in the stock of an up-and-coming company that you believe in. No matter what it is, you should study it, create an account with the proper financial institution, put a healthy but not overwhelming amount into that investment, and then watch it grow.

Don't make emotional, knee-jerk reactions and make sure that you take your time, remain cautious and smart, and don't jump at shadows in the marketplace.

Investing can be a huge benefit to your financial standing and your personal finance but you have to do it the right way. Take some time to start reading business blogs and headlines and learn even more about the world of investing because it really can be a great way to add excitement - and more money - to your young life.

Next Steps

The first step to starting your investing journey is a fun one: find out what makes you passionate.

Are you excited about the blossoming world of cryptocurrency? Do you like the concept of NFTs? Have you always had an itch to participate with the stock market on Wall Street?

You need to think hard about which sort of investment is something you can get fired up and excited for. Because one of the key things to remember about investing is that you should only do it if you believe in what you're putting your money into.

Remember that investing is a long-term project, it is something you will have to commit to. That is all the more reason why you should try to figure out which sort of commodity and project you can happily put your money into.

There are many investment opportunities out there, especially now. Which one feels right and exhilarating to you? Once you know that, you can then set up an account or inquire about putting your money into.

So, that's your first step: what do *you* want to invest in?

Step 6:
Getting Multiple Sources Of Income

We live in what people call the "gig economy."

Essentially, what this means is that millions of people don't make money the old-fashioned way, where they show up at a nine-to-five job where they clock in, clock out, and receive a paycheck like people have for generations.

Instead, some people are actually making money in new and exciting ways. Maybe they are delivering food from local restaurants. Maybe they are running a blog. Maybe they have a YouTube channel that generates money for them via advertisements.

And maybe they are doing this *on top* of having a more traditional, regular job. There are millions of young people who are doing just that: they are making money in multiple ways at the same time. This means that they are able to pursue interests that they are passionate about and are able to actually turn a buck by doing so.

When you are young and looking to earn a decent amount of money and gain control of your personal finance, earning multiple streams of income is a very smart thing to do. It will help you have a robust bank account, a lot of opportunities and experiences, and the ability to do what you love.

By getting multiple sources of income, you can not only live more comfortably, but you can follow the pursuits that really make you happy. You can actually make money by being creative and doing the things you love. What could be better than that?

Innovative Ways To Make Extra Income

Why would you possibly want multiple streams of income coming into your bank account?

Perhaps, unfortunately, the job that you are working isn't paying enough or working you often to make ends meet. Maybe you are struggling to get by and you need to gain another source of money so that you can pay rent. That's a very legitimate reason why many people seek a second source of income.

But maybe you are wanting to make some extra money because you have available hours at the end of the day that you can devote to earning some cash. Maybe you have a lot of youthful energy and a drive to create, work hard, and lay forth a foundation for your financial future.

By getting a second source of income, you can set yourself up well for many years to come. If you have the energy, the drive, and the time, you can add multiple sources of income that will only pad your bank account and create funds for vacations, fun expenditures, and more.

You can live a fun life when you are making some extra money for yourself and your well-being and future. But what are some of the best, smartest, most innovative ways to have extra incomes? Now more than ever, the possibilities are exciting, unique, and seemingly endless.

Freelancing

What is freelancing? It's someone who provides any different type of service to multiple clients. If you want to be a freelancer you can be someone who writes, who reads and edits, who draws, who paints, who records his or her voice, and any number of things. Practically any sort of job can be found through freelancing.

So, if you're looking to do freelance work, how do you find clients that will hire you? That's easy! There are multiple websites, such as Upwork, Freelancer, Fiverr, and more that allow you to build a freelance profile, reach out to employers, and make the connections needed to land jobs. You'll have to have a portfolio of previous work ready to go to find clients and you'll need to make sure you sell yourself well. But no matter what sort of freelance work you want to tackle, these sorts of websites will help you make your side hustle dream a reality.

Blogging

Blogging is a lot of fun! In fact, you have probably had at least one blog at one point in your life. But did you know that blogging could become a side hustle that pays you handsomely?

Indeed, blogging is a great way to make some money but it does take time. It starts with an idea. You need to figure out what sort of blog you are wanting to run. What fascinates you? What do you have a lot of knowledge about? In other words, what is something that you can write about often with expertise and voice and in ways that will attract a reading audience.

Then you need to start your blog and write consistently. And you need to find an audience. This can be done via creating a Facebook or social media page, reaching out to other blogs, or even advertising a bit on other sites. But it's vital that you find people who will read your page regularly because that is key to making some money.

The way that you turn blogging into a proper side hustle is via advertising. Through Google and other sites and companies that provide ads, you will be able to post advertisements on your blog. But this will only pay off after you've blogged for a while and after you have established a reliable audience too. Therefore, it's all the more important to make sure you are writing well and in a way that is bringing readers in.

Proofread

When you see an ad or press release or any sort of written content, via Facebook or the newspaper or on a billboard - or really anywhere - you are seeing content that has moved through a long list of people who have all had a hand in making it 100% ready for public consumption.

A major part of that process is proofreading. Without proofreading, there would be errors, grammatical embarrassments, and an overall sense that the content just doesn't make sense. For years now, proofreaders have been the unsung heroes of nearly every industry. And you can be one!

If you want to start a side hustle as a proofreader, you'll need a few things. Firstly, you need to set up some sort of website to advertise yourself. Think of this as a calling card or billboard. Find some companies or even friends who you can proofread for - for free! Whether it be a literary paper or an ad, just do the work for them with the promise that if they are happy with your work, they will give you a quote for your website. Perfect! Now you have people who will recommend you.

Now you need to reach out to smaller, local businesses. Ask them what they need when it comes to proofreading, show them your website, the rave reviews, and foster a relationship with them. Don't push too hard! But let them know if they need *any* sort of proofreading work, you are ready and eager.

You won't get paid a whole lot of money for each job but it will build up over time and you can get more clients if you do a good job. There are many pluses to being a proofreader too. It's in fact a great side hustle because of these benefits.

Tutoring Online

Were you the type of student who did a great job at teaching others? If so, tutoring could be the right approach for you to make some extra money. Indeed, tutoring is the sort of side hustle that is making many people a lot of money and the best part about it is that there is *always* a need for a tutor somewhere.

We all know how tutoring works. You will meet with a student and focus on a given subject they're having trouble with. It may be English, Math, Science, or more. Obviously, you need to be very well-versed in whatever subjects you are going to tutor about. It would be best if you had a degree in said subject. For example, if you're going to tutor someone and teach them about writing, an English degree would be an excellent way to convince someone to use your services.

Finding someone to tutor is a little difficult at times. Many people turn to sites such as Craigslist to create ads and find potential clients. That's a great approach but there are other options too. Many people are now building Facebook pages devoted to tutoring side hustles. Whatever approach you take, make sure it looks professional. Remember that the clientele you'll be attracting are mostly parents and they aren't going to be willing to spend money on someone who doesn't seem to know what they're doing.

Ridesharing

Nearly all of us have called upon the assistance of Uber or Lyft at one point or another and the people who work for that company have found that they can turn a pretty penny by doing so.

Sign up to drive for either of these companies if you want to make extra money, whenever you want. Perhaps you can do it after a long shift at your day job. Maybe you can do it on your days off. Maybe you can do it in the dead of night when you can't sleep.

The great thing about doing rideshare work is that you get to make your own schedule, you get to work whenever you want. You are not beholden to a special schedule and you can clock in and clock out whenever you want.

Literally millions of people have signed up to do rideshare work and they have made a lot of money, met many people, and had great experiences. And they have done all of it when they choose, not stuck to a rigid schedule that doesn't allow for a personal life and another job.

Why Do You Want Multiple Sources Of Income?

Some people have enough on their plates by just working their regular jobs. There are not enough hours in the day for extra sources of income for these people.

That's completely fine and totally understandable too. However, there are many young people your age who *are* willing to work more and pad their bank accounts with extra funds via the jobs listed above - and many more.

And why do you want extra streams of income funneling into your bank account? Well, the biggest reason is that you can give yourself true financial security when you do this.

You never know what might be right around the corner, you don't know what sort of surprises - both good and bad - that life holds for you. When you have more than a single income stream, you will have something that you can turn to and rely upon if hard times fall upon you. If you lose your main job, then one of these multiple sources of income will help you survive and get by. It will get rid of stress and it will also make you feel far more comfortable if you hit a rough patch.

But multiple sources of income will also help you pay down any form of debt you may have accumulated. Perhaps you are trying to pay off your student debt or some other amount that you have racked up in your youthful, carefree years. That isn't the end of the world, many people have done that.

Multiple sources of income will help you pay off whatever amount you owe to others. This will allow you to live off of the money you make with your first job, while the money you gain from multiple extra streams of income will let you pay off debts and live a financially healthy life.

Last, but certainly not least, extra income streams will let you have more fun in life - and everyone wants that. Now you will be able to go on that trip you have wanted, or buy that new smartphone you've desired, or enjoy some fancy dinners with friends and family and buy the best birthday gifts for the people you love.

Next Steps

It's time for you to make multiple sources of income. But, how? What's the first thing you should do?

The good news here is that earning multiple income sources has never been easier. You can start doing one of the recommended jobs as soon as possible, even within the span of a few hours. For example, you can start your blog today and you can sign up for DoorDash, Uber, or Lyft this very afternoon.

Therefore, here is what you should do: simply hop on the respective website for the job that you want and you can start getting to work at making this a new source of income for you. It isn't that hard because each of these companies are looking for hard-working, determined young people who are willing and ready to get out there and get going.

Do you want multiple sources of income so that you can enjoy life better and have a fuller bank account and a more comfortable existence? Well, there is now nothing holding you back.

Step 7:
Financial Freedom

"Financial stability is much more about doing the best with what you have and not about achieving a certain level of income."
— *Erik Wecks*

What is financial freedom and why is it the last - and possibly most important - step to experiencing true personal finance expertise in your young life?

Financial freedom is exactly what it sounds like: it is being free of debt, making smart investments, having cash to carry around and enjoy yourself with, and also holding multiple options and opportunities for your future.

But just knowing what financial freedom is doesn't mean you can achieve it. We have gone over many of the steps needed to live a life with strong personal finance and responsibility and health but let's go over the most important things to keep in mind when you are attempting to have real, true financial freedom.

By remembering these things, you can create a path for yourself that is free of the pitfalls that usually hurt so many people, empty their bank accounts, create headaches, and have them borrowing money and barely making ends meet.

Set Your Goals

You need to know what you want.

You have probably heard this before but it's especially true when you are trying to live a life of financial freedom. Sometimes you will need to know exactly what you want (for example, are you trying to buy a new car?) and sometimes you will have a vague idea of what you want (maybe you tell yourself you want to travel more).

But goals are always important, whether they be concrete and set in stone or ambiguous and general. If you don't know what you want, you can't achieve it. If you *do* know what you're aiming for, you can then begin budgeting, saving, making money, and then making plans to achieve your goals.

Don't Overspend

Has anyone ever told you to live below your means?

This is a common expression that people share that basically means you shouldn't be overspending and going crazy with the money that you are using. That's solid, sound advice that you should always follow, especially when you are young and just starting out your adult life.

If you live a frugal lifestyle, you will find that you always have more money in your pocket, or your bank account to be more precise. You will also notice that this might take some practice but it will soon be a mindset that you will feel throughout all of your day. You will be more relaxed and with less stress and less anxiety too.

Living below your means doesn't mean you have to only be eating rice every single night. You can still enjoy yourself and some of the finer things in life. But you won't be spending cash you don't have to and you won't be finding yourself out of money by the time your rent payment is due.

Take Care Of Your Health

If you want to have true financial freedom, you need to take great pains to make sure that you are always as healthy as can be.

You might not think about it but bad health can lead to a bad balance in your bank account and it's something to come back from.

If you don't take care of yourself and grow sick, you will need to see a medical professional and that will cost you a pretty penny, especially if you don't have health insurance. Additionally, getting really sick will mean that you aren't able to work as much and that will lessen the amount of your paychecks and could really compromise your position at work overall.

Everyone always says that an apple a day keeps the doctor away, but it also keeps the bill collectors away as well.

Make It A Habit

Perhaps the most important thing to remember when you are trying to find financial freedom for yourself is to make these positive changes you have pursued into habits.

Don't just do these things one time, do them regularly. For example, many people will go days without checking their bank account and seeing how much is in there and what bills and payments are coming due within the next few weeks. But that won't be you. Instead, you will be checking regularly - even once a day. By doing so, you will stay on top of your own financial well-being and will always know what you have, don't have, and what is on the horizon for you.

But you can't just do this one time. You need to do this regularly. The same is true for budgeting, or not overspending, or checking the health of your investments. All of these things need to become a regular part of your life, something you do often.

Before long, you will see that you have turned each of these concepts into habits that you are doing without thinking. They will be second nature, and your financial well-being and freedom will only grow stronger for years to come.

Financial freedom is all about standing on your own. There are many ways to do this. And the good news is that there are very few *wrong* ways to do it. The ideas given above are just the ones that are best to get started but there are many things you can do to master your personal finance.

Next Steps

How do you get started on this as soon as possible? It's plain and easy to do: start setting your goals. You are young, you have your whole life before you, and you know you want to achieve great things. So, what is the biggest goal you want to achieve within the next year? Take a look at that and then start making a plan. This is the first step of many that will soon have you on a path of financial freedom.

This is a fun first step. Writing down your goals is a great way to think long and hard about how you want to reward yourself and the sort of life you want to live.

You cannot know what you are working for unless you know what you want. Your next step should be to think about your life over the next year and try to figure out what you want to achieve, what you want to buy, and the sort of life you want to live. Paint a picture in your mind of your goals and then you can start achieving them.

Conclusion

"Being rich is having money; being wealthy is having time."
— Margaret Bonnano

There are many ways to *not* have good personal finance and there are many ways to have good personal finance too.

Accumulating a good, solid, healthy bank account is a lot of work and it can take years upon years of planning, dedication, budgeting, saving, and tweaking your plans again and again. But here is the good news: you are young and you have all the time in the world - at least right now.

Just because you still have your whole life ahead of you doesn't mean that you shouldn't be paying attention to your finances and getting a handle on how to control them, enhance them, keep them safe, and plot a path ahead into the future.

The truth is that you're never too young to be thinking about your personal finances and what lies ahead for you. If you ask most billionaires or successful business people, they will say that they wish they had started taking finances seriously way earlier in their lives.

You have the luxury of time. You have the luxury of energy too. You are not currently bogged down by the many things that slow other people down. There are people twice your age who look back and wish that they had done things differently. They wish that they had saved more. They wish they learned how to budget. They wish that they had taken the advice of others and invested in something that could have made them so much money.

You can do all of that. You can save money, you can budget, you can invest, you can see your finances blossom into so much more. By the time you are 30 years old, you can be quite comfortable with your finances - but only if you do the work.

We have gone over so many different things that will help you maintain strong and healthy personal finances and, as you can see, they all take a good deal of work and dedication. Sometimes you have to change the way you think, other times you have to try new things.

But always you have to stay dedicated and keep one goal in mind: you want to be financially free and you want the sort of personal finance skills that will allow you to live a comfortable life. Maybe you're not planning on becoming a millionaire but you are planning on not having to worry about your bank account, waiting anxiously for each paycheck just to make ends meet.

That is easily attainable if you follow the advice and steps we have gone through in this book. Yes, some of the things we have touched upon will take time and even some hard work but, again, you have the time and you have the energy.

So many young people go out into the world looking to live wildly, quickly, and with a lot of fun every night. They are looking to often make memories that will last a lifetime. Well, you can do that too while *still* working on your personal finances too. You can have a great time and live a wonderful young life and still make sure that you have a masterful hold on your money and the way that you spend, save, budget, and plan ahead.

In fact, you can have even more fun if you are doing that. You can enjoy yourself even more. You can make even better memories, all because you are doing what needs to be done to keep your personal finance issues in order.

Money is important. No matter what people say, it really does make the world go around. Why wouldn't you want to understand and deftly handle something that is so vital to a long, happy, exciting life?

Exclusive 5-day bonus course just for you!

We will be sharing the top adulting tips and life hacks you absolutely need to know in order to set yourself up for success.

Simply let us know where to send the course e-mails to via this link below.

https://bit.ly/jerrell-mccain

Redeem your free audiobook by e-mailing us at bookgrowthpublishing@mail.com **(limited redemptions)**

Made in the USA
Las Vegas, NV
20 October 2023

79408701R00080